BEAT STRE

Dr Bill Munro MBChB, MFOM, MFCH, DPH, DIH, DTM&H qualified in Edinburgh in 1952. As a student, he was President of the University Union. For fifteen years he was senior partner of a large private practice in Malaya.

Returning to the UK he specialized in community medicine before joining the pharmaceutical industry, where he became Medical Director of a major company. In 1981 he was appointed Regional Medical Director for the Post Office.

Frances Munro is a pharmacologist and worked in clinical research and management for several major pharmaceutical companies. She has a diploma in counselling.

Bill and Frances have two sons and live in Sussex, where they run SALT – the Stress And Life Trust.

Beat Stress

A 30-DAY PROGRAMME
FOR LIVING SUCCESSFULLY

Dr Bill Munro and
Frances Munro

Marshall Pickering
An Imprint of HarperCollins*Publishers*

Marshall Pickering is an Imprint of
HarperCollins*Religious*
Part of HarperCollins*Publishers*
77–85 Fulham Palace Road
Hammersmith, London W6 8JB

First published in Great Britain
in 1993 by Marshall Pickering

10 9 8 7 6 5 4 3 2 1

A catalogue record for this book is
available from the British Library

ISBN 0 551 02759-2

Printed and bound in Great Britain by
HarperCollinsManufacturing Glasgow

Contents

Foreword
By Jennifer Rees Larcombe

Perhaps most of us Christians feel stress is 'unspiritual' and some kind of a failure. After all, Jesus came to give us His peace and 'life in all its fullness' (John 10:10). Yet life today is very stressful, particularly for people who try to pack church activities and helping others on top of job commitments and family pressures.

This book was such a relief to me because it does not condemn us for being human and feeling pressured. Bill says, 'People who come to us suffering from stress problems often say to us, "But I'm a Christian. I shouldn't feel anxious or depressed. I feel guilty about this and it's making me feel even more stressed." But we have to acknowledge that, though born again and filled with the Spirit we are still human. We will not be perfect until we join the Lord Jesus . . . Naturally we will feel anxious if we are about to lose our job. We will feel sad and will want to grieve if we lose a loved one. We will feel hurt if friends let us down or reject us.'

But the reason I found this book such a help was that it does not only sympathize it reminds us that as Christians we do not have to be crushed and destroyed by these things. There is a way we can cope with the stress of life and it goes on to show us how in a simple and straightforward way.

I first met the Munros at a time when I was beginning to suffer from the effects of stress. No serious disasters were hitting my life, it wasn't that things were going wrong, it was just that too many things were going right – all at once – and I couldn't stretch the hours of each day far enough to cope with all the clamouring demands. I felt embarrassed when I realized my body was creaking and protesting at all the demands I was making upon it –

the late nights, early mornings and long hours travelling. It felt humiliating to find my brain whirling like a speeded-up cement mixer as I forced it to think of too many things at once. 'Christians shouldn't feel like this', I told myself miserably as I set off to speak at a conference for women in full-time work for God. It was there that I met Frances – she was to take a seminar on stress. 'I'd better come and hear you', I told her ruefully.

The sheer down-to-earth commonsense of all she said impressed me greatly, and I think for many of us who were there, that seminar was a life-changing experience. As she was speaking I realized what had been going wrong for me. Like Peter I had taken my eyes off Jesus and was looking at the tossing waves instead. I was reminded that as a Christian I might well be surrounded by the unavoidable storms of life – the activities, pressures and sorrows – but I did not need to be drowned by them, so long as I kept on putting my trust in Christ.

In this book Bill and Frances break down the concepts they teach in their Seminars into simple daily steps. When you are feeling stressed up to the eye-balls the last thing you want to do is read a book on the subject. But the joy of this book is that you don't have to read it! Anyway, not all at once. I found it so helpful just being able to go through it a few pages each day, giving myself time to rethink my priorities and absorb all the practical tips and suggestions.

Sometimes when life is really being tough it is hard to pray, and you can't seem to think where to look in the Bible to find the help you need. So the beautiful little prayers and relevant verses for each day are a very good idea indeed. I also loved the humour! They say laughter is the best medicine, and some of the stories and statements in the book made me weep with laughter – a real tonic.

The shops are full of books which tell us how to look after our bodies. There are also many which feed our minds academically. Others build us spiritually and help us see things from God's perspective. But this is the first book I've found which does all three things at once and treats us as whole human beings. We all know we have a body, a mind and a spirit, but usually we treat them as three separate compartments, unrelated to each other.

This book helped me to see how very closely related all three of my 'departments' really are and how much the health of each one affects the well being of the other two.

It would be a great shame if people did not read this book until they were beginning to 'suffer' from stress. Prevention is better than cure, so I believe it is a must for all busy people. While it is an excellent step-by-step method of beating stress it is an equally excellent step-by-step guide to becoming a whole human being, fit and healthy in body, mind and spirit.

Tunbridge Wells
February 1993

A 30-day plan not only for beating stress but for living successfully

This is a 'how to' book – a day-to-day, step-by-step, practical guide to beating stress and living successfully. It applies Christian teaching and beliefs to findings from stress research.

Preliminaries

We hope you enjoy reading the manual, but *reading alone will not change your life*. The instructions and advice have to be followed and become part of your daily living. Reading books about Beethoven and listening to his wonderful music may inspire us, but we will have to spend hours every day practising the violin if we ever hope to play that instrument sweetly, let alone like a virtuoso.

An athlete will not get very far if he merely reads about what he should do. Have you been impressed by those who want to do well in sport, how seriously they take their training, how they apply themselves, and how much they are prepared to practise? Life is the most important race you will ever run. If you mean business about living successfully, then it must be worth while spending time

STUDYING, APPLYING and PRACTISING

the correct principles.

This is why the course is divided into thirty short sections, each easy to read, follow and put into practice.

While it is a 30-DAY-PLAN you may find that you need to take more than one day to master certain elements. We would strongly advise that you stay with each day until you feel that it has become part of your life before moving on to the next day. If then it takes you more than thirty days to finish the course, don't worry. Better to have mastered each section rather than to press on willy nilly.

One other tip: if your mornings are rushed getting off to work in time, or getting the children out to school, it will probably be better for you to read through and digest a day's section the day or evening before, making your own brief notes of what you have to remember and do the next day. These notes can then be read through quickly and followed when the day arrives.

IT IS VERY IMPORTANT that any medical conditions are dealt with or are being dealt with before embarking on the course. If you have not recently had a medical check-up, if you are not sure about your fitness, or if you are currently on medication, then it is wise to get clearance from your GP before starting the course.

The programme itself

We are made up of three parts – body, soul and spirit. We must give attention to all three if we are going to function at our best and so be able to cope with the pressures of life.

DAYS 1–30 deal with important issues of body and soul.

THE THREE COUNTDOWN DAYS (−3, −2, −1) deal with the spirit from a Christian point of view. Because of the paramount importance of the spirit, the preparatory work in these three days lays the foundation for you to get the very best out of the 30-day-plan.

IF YOU THEN STUDY, FOLLOW AND *PUT INTO PRACTICE* THE DAILY SECRETS WE SHARE WITH YOU, YOU CAN BEGIN NOT JUST TO COPE BUT REALLY TO LIVE LIFE TO THE FULL!

PART ONE

Countdown

Day −3

A new beginning

'I WOULD REALLY LIKE TO STOP AND START ALL OVER AGAIN.' Have you ever felt or said this? Many of the people we see with stress problems say this to us.

The wonderful news in the Bible is that anyone can have a new beginning.

If you have made this new beginning by becoming a Christian in the past, then now, in preparation for the course, is an opportunity to remind yourself of what it means to you.

YOU HAVE BEEN COMPLETELY FORGIVEN

for all your past. What a relief to know that all guilt has been swept away. God does not even remember the bad things, the faults, the sins of commission and omission. So there is no need for you to dwell on them or keep bringing them up in your mind – or in your prayers. If God has forgiven you, then *you can forgive yourself!*

YOU RECEIVED A BRAND NEW SPIRIT FROM GOD,

which is like a newborn baby – perfect, undamaged and full of new and eternal life. How wonderful to know that you are *a new creation*.

YOU WILL LIVE FOR EVER WITH GOD.

Any fear you had of death has been replaced by this assurance.

5

In other words, your new beginning has taken care of the past, the present and the future.

If you have not had this new beginning then GOD CAN OFFER IT TO YOU NOW – before you begin the course, with all that He guarantees going with it. But like every offer and guarantee, there are conditions.

If you can pray the words below and really mean them, then this new beginning can be yours today.

> *Dear God,*
>
> *I admit that I have done wrong. I have been going my own way rather than yours. I have not been putting you first in my life, and because of this I deserve to die. I believe that Jesus Christ is your Son, that He came to earth and died in my place and that He rose again from the dead.*
>
> *I am sorry for my past and ask you to forgive me. I now want to go your way and put my life in your hands. I accept your forgiveness, your gift of a brand new human spirit and your Holy Spirit to live in my spirit.*
>
> *In Jesus's name, Amen.*

There is more good news and it can save you from stress and worry in the future. Once you have received the new spirit it cannot be taken away – it is there for keeps. Your new spirit has been born of the Spirit of God. It has been re-born – and

YOU CANNOT BE UNBORN!

So no matter how much you feel, or will feel in the future, that you have blown it, gone back to square one and so on, whatever happens, the new spirit is yours.

NOTHING CAN TAKE YOUR NEW SPIRIT AWAY.

Thoughts for today

- For God so loved the world that He gave His one and only Son, that whoever believes in Him shall not perish but have eternal life. (John 3:16)
- Jesus declared '. . . no one can see the Kingdom of God unless he is born again.' (John 3:3)
- Therefore, if anyone is in Christ, he is a new creation; the old has gone, the new has come! (2 Corinthians 5:17)

A new start − what then?

We saw yesterday that a new beginning is possible and that once you have received a new spirit it cannot be taken away.

But having made a completely new start with the slate wiped clean − what then?

Because it is a PERFECT new spirit − a new creation of God's − you cannot do anything to make it better. You cannot improve on it.

HOWEVER − YOUR NEW SPIRIT CAN GROW, DEVELOP AND MATURE.

A beautiful flower cannot be improved but it can grow and flourish and develop. Since your spirit is the most important part of you it should be tended and nurtured and nourished.

Many people look after their bodies, being careful how they eat and how they exercise and work out. Many look after their souls and minds with analysis and counselling and therapy. Many completely ignore their spirits. If you neglect your spirit then it will be stunted and maturity will be delayed.

If you want your spirit to grow and develop then you must tend it in a number of ways.

1. *Time with God*

A few years ago we suggested to our house group that we all go off to different parts of the house or garden, and sit, walk or stand for half an hour in God's presence. We were not to spend the time praying or reading our Bible but simply to have a sense of Jesus sitting or standing or walking with us – so that we were in His company. If He spoke to us – great, but if He also only wanted to be with us, not necessarily to speak to us or have us speak to Him, then that was fine.

When we came together after half an hour, all agreed that it was the best house group we had ever had. Perhaps we should not have been surprised that people were thrilled to have become aware of Jesus's presence and to have spent some time with Him, rather than listening to our teaching or even praying for each other.

Much of the time we seek God's hand: His hand to guide us; His hand to provide for us; His hand to protect us; His hand to heal us. It is important that sometimes we seek His FACE – just to know He is there, that He is looking at us.

WHEN DID YOU LAST SPEND TIME ALONE WITH JESUS? – YOUR SPIRIT COMMUNING WITH HIS SPIRIT?

When you do – it will do your spirit a world of good!

2. Worship

This can be done alone, anywhere, at any time: when we worship who God is; when we wonder at His might, His holiness, His love, His wisdom, and tell Him how much He means to us.

But often worship will be with a number of His people, in His church.

There is, we believe, some misconception about why we meet together as Christians, for example on a Sunday. It should be primarily to worship God. We may be taught, and learn from His word, and we may receive a blessing, but the main purpose should be to worship the Lord Jesus.

This may be in music, in singing, in speech, in dance, or in silence.

When we bear this in mind, understand why we are doing it and enter into the worship and enjoy it, attending church takes on a whole new meaning.

Perhaps, like us, you have wondered why we are told to

worship God. What kind of God is this who wants us to bow down and worship Him? He has instructed us to do this because He knows how much it will benefit us, will benefit our spirit.

There may be times when you don't feel particularly like singing or worshipping. It is even more important, at such times, that by an act of will you start worshipping, for as you do, your spirit will rise and be refreshed.

3. Bible reading and study

Through this, you will learn more about God: who He is; what He is like; and His purposes for you. New things, revelation and old well-known passages and texts, and how they do not change, will speak to your spirit.

4. Prayer

It is important that your prayers are not just lists of requests, or even lists of confessions, important as both of these are. But as you open up your heart to Him, tell Him of your joys and sorrows, successes and failures, and listen to Him – prayer should be a two-way process – and hear His voice of forgiveness, acceptance, understanding, love, compassion and encouragement – your spirit will rise.

5. Meditation

Meditating – without thinking actively, or praying actively – on God's word and on Him do wonders for our spirit.

TENDING, FEEDING, NURTURING AND EXERCISING YOUR SPIRIT (as you do your body), WILL MAKE IT GROW, DEVELOP AND MATURE.

Action this day

1 PLAN TIME – actually put it in your diary – to spend time with Jesus.
2 RESOLVE to go to church on Sunday with the express and main purpose of worshipping God.
3 BUY or order daily Bible study notes. Plan time to read a Bible passage each day.
4 DECIDE when you are going to spend time daily in prayer. Start with a short time – for example, five minutes (not much out of twenty-four hours) as the target. You can lengthen it as and when you want to.
5 SWITCH OFF the TV some time today and spend five minutes meditating on words from the Bible or on God Himself.

Thoughts for today

- Your face, Lord, I will seek. (Psalm 27:8)
- You will fill me with joy in your presence. (Psalm 16:11)
- Jesus answered, 'It is written "Worship the Lord your God and serve Him only"'.
- All scripture is God-breathed . . . so that the man of God may be thoroughly equipped for every good work. (2 Timothy 3:16, 17)
- Pray continually. (1 Thessalonians 5:17)
- For the eyes of the Lord are on the righteous and his ears are attentive to their prayer. (1 Peter 3:12)
- Blessed is the man whose delight is in the law of the Lord, and on His law he meditates day and night. He is like a tree planted by streams of water, which yields its fruit in season and whose leaf does not wither. Whatever he does prospers. (Psalm 1:2, 3)

The secret of living successfully

If you have made a new start – been born again – then:

1 You have been totally forgiven and have booked your passage to heaven; and
2 You have a new spirit, which, if you put into regular practice the actions outlined yesterday, is set to grow.

A third thing has happened, God's own Spirit – the Holy Spirit – has taken up resident in your spirit. Are you aware of this?

THE GOD OF THE UNIVERSE NOW LIVES IN YOUR SPIRIT IN A SUPERNATURAL WAY.

As your spirit grows and as you learn to 'tune in' to the Holy Spirit – your conscience becomes more sensitive, and you begin to be aware of the 'promptings' of the Holy Spirit to think and speak and do things. If you expect this to happen, then it will, more and more, as each day passes.

Now for the real secret of living successfully

During the next thirty days you will learn what stress research has discovered can make you less vulnerable to pressures; but much more than that, you will learn what God, your maker, advises to enable you to live successfully. If you want to get the most out of your car or computer then if wise you will go by the maker's manual. Similarly, if you want to get the most out of your life it is sensible to follow *your* maker's instructions – in the Bible.

Unfortunately some makers' manuals are difficult to understand fully or to follow. In fact, sometimes the Bible seems to turn things on their head and the advice is at odds with what we would naturally believe.

However, the Holy Spirit, who now lives in your spirit, can open the eyes of your mind so that you will see what the instructions mean, and in fact that they do make sense.

So before going further, why not ask Him to do just that for you by praying:

Please, Holy Spirit, open the eyes of my mind so that I will understand and be able to believe that what your manual says is true, and that what I will learn from it will work in my life. Amen.

Without this, although some of the guidelines will appear sensible, others will seem absolutely crazy and in some cases the exact opposite of how you normally think. The Holy Spirit will amazingly let you see things differently and will help you to understand properly.

Unfortunately, at this stage what may happen is as follows. Some people, having been born again, and having been shown by the Holy Spirit what is needed to become followers of Jesus Christ, to follow the Bible's teachings and to live successfully – to become good Christians, in other words – begin to try ever so hard to be and do all that they should.

Living the new Christian life becomes very hard and difficult, and there are so many failures that these Christians think they are never going to be more than second-rate Christians. They may feel like giving up, and may sometimes even wish that they had never started on this path. At least before they started they did not get all frustrated and depressed because they did not fully know what would be required of them.

In a way, they are like the children of Israel who have escaped from Egypt – they are now free but are finding life difficult, without much to shout about as they wander around in the wilderness. Some even begin to wish that they were back in Egypt where, although they had not been free, life in some ways was easier.

If you feel that you are in the 'wilderness' and that the Christian life is a terrible slog, then there is an answer for you. Or, if you feel that you want to go through with this course, but are afraid that it may turn out to be full of trying, with scant success and a lot of discouragement, just like all the other times you have turned over a new leaf – then take heart.

GOD DID NOT WANT THE ISRAELITES TO REMAIN IN THE WILDERNESS. HE WANTED THEM TO GET ON INTO THE PROMISED LAND.

In the same way

HE WANTS YOU TO LIVE SUCCESSFULLY IN HIS KINGDOM AND TO LEAVE THE WILDERNESS BEHIND.

There will still be struggles ahead, just as there were for the Israelites in the promised land, but

SUCCESS WAS ASSURED FOR THEM AND IT IS FOR YOU.

You can enter the 'promised land' now – today, before starting the main part of the course – knowing that

YOU WILL BE ABLE TO SUCCEED DAILY AND LEARN TO BEAT STRESS.

Here's the secret

Do you remember what the disciples were like? For a time – when Jesus was with them – they healed and preached and followed Him despite some setbacks. But when the real test came – when Jesus was betrayed, captured, accused and crucified – they all got scared, gave up and ran off. And that's where it might have ended for them, in disillusionment and defeat, had it not been for the coming of the Holy Spirit.

Jesus had promised that, when He rose again and went back to His Father, He would send the Holy Spirit and they should wait in Jerusalem till He came. This they did – and you can read in the Acts of the Apostles (chapters 1 and 2) what happpened. The Holy Spirit did come as Jesus had promised and He filled the disciples. From then on they were changed men. From a fearful, scared and beaten lot, they became real men and went out to tell everyone boldly about Jesus and to live successfully.

The difference was the Holy Spirit. God wants you to stop trying in your own strength, in your own way. He wants to fight the battles for you. He can and He will . . .

. . . IF YOU LET HIM. He has provided the Holy Spirit to empower you. His life and power can be yours. His plan is not to support you from the outside, like some kind of scaffolding helping to shore you up, nor basically is it to help you to do things, but rather that His Holy Spirit will live within you and work through you. His plan is not only for His Spirit to live in your spirit, but to FILL YOUR SOUL – how you think, feel and act – so that His life becomes yours.

Do you want your soul to be filled with God's Spirit, with His power and love and wisdom replacing your weakness, lack of love and foolishness? Who in his or her right mind would not?

If you do, two important steps are involved.

1 You will only be filled to the extent that you are willing to empty yourself. That's only common sense. You can do this by praying from your heart:

Lord Jesus, I want to die to self. I no longer want to do things my way, how I think, and feel and behave. I place all my life and future, all my assets and all my debits [it can help to list here all the important things you depend upon in your life – see Action this day] in your hands and relinquish all my rights to them.

2 You then have to ask God to fill you with His Spirit, or ask another Christian to ask this for you – by praying

Lord Jesus, now that I have emptied myself I ask you to fill me to overflowing with your Holy Spirit.

Some people feel a real surge of power at this moment and a real lightening of their load. Some feel ecstatic. Some feel a tremendous peace coming over them. Others may not feel anything at that moment. BUT REST ASSURED – if you really have placed all in His hands and have asked to be filled, then you ARE now supernaturally filled with God's Spirit.

YOU ARE READY TO BENEFIT FROM THE REST OF THIS COURSE, AND READY FOR WHATEVER LIFE BRINGS TO YOU.

Prayer

Lord Jesus,
Thank you for filling me with your Holy Spirit, with all that this can mean for my life. I now wait, with great expectancy, to see your power and wisdom at work in my life and flowing out to others.

Please show me whenever I take things back under my own control and power so that I can relinquish them to you, so that I can stay filled with your Spirit. Amen.

Action this day

1 Ask God to show you all the things that you have to give up rights to if you want to be completely filled with His Holy Spirit.
2 List all of these things – the good and the bad – and then give them over to God.
3 Resolve to review your life each day – especially noting the things you have taken back from God before making them over to Him again.

Thoughts for today

- Jesus said, 'You will receive power when the Holy Spirit comes on you.' (Acts 1:8)
- They were all filled with the Holy Spirit and spoke the word of God boldly. (Acts 4:31)
- His divine power has given us everything we need for life and godliness. (2 Peter 1:3)
- Jesus said, 'If anyone would come after me, he must deny himself and take up his cross [lose control of his life] and follow me. For whoever wants to save his life will lose it, and whoever loses his life for me will find it.' (Matthew 16:24, 25)

PART TWO

The 30-day plan

Day 1

How to relax

A very powerful but simple relaxation technique

This course is not just about being calm or at peace, or being able to relax. It is about much more – it's about beating stress and living successfully.

However, you are going to find it much easier to take in and practise the daily programme if you are relaxed, rather than tense and unable to wind down; and if you are rested and sleeping well, rather than tired and on edge from disturbed nights.

A relaxation technique may help, and there are many available, some more effective than others. Some are difficult to learn and some are unacceptable to Christians because of their possible association with the occult, New Age, or Eastern religions.

Some Christians believe that a relaxation technique should not be necessary, since they should be able to relax and be at peace without one – and we respect this view. However, we do believe that some people need help, and a 'good' technique must be better than taking minor tranquillizers (such as diazepam) and sleeping pills which affect the brain and can become very addictive.

We are going to share with you the basics of a simple, yet very powerful technique which we have taught to many thousands of patients over the past twelve years. These have included people from many different backgrounds, amongst them sportsmen, business executives, policemen, teachers, housewives, other counsellors – both Christian and secular – and many clergymen and church leaders. All have benefited and none has felt that there was anything unwholesome in the technique. There is no religious or quasi-religious connotation in it.

HOWEVER – IF YOU FEEL THAT SUCH A TECHNIQUE IS NOT FOR YOU THEN, MOVE ON NOW TO DAY TWO.

Many other techniques involve listening to a tape and in a way are a form of hypnosis, even if they do not specifically use hypnosis. But this technique you will actually practise yourself. You will be learning to help yourself. So if you are one of those people who want to be involved in your own health (and we think you must be, since you are reading this book) rather than relying on popping pills or having things done for you, then this technique should appeal to you. Here is a little more background about it:

1 We and many of our counsellees have tried other relaxation techniques but have found this the most powerful of all.
2 This is more than a simple relaxation technique. The exercises will not only calm your mind and body but quite rapidly begin to allow you to think more clearly and rationally, so that you can start facing up to problems and dealing with them.
3 The exercises affect your body through the autonomic nervous system so that, for example, your heart and breathing slow down and your blood pressure falls.

Your brain and brain waves are also affected. It is important therefore that if you have been under medical or psychiatric treatment in the past, and particularly if you are currently on *any* medication, you consult your GP or specialist before starting these exercises. They should not have any damaging effect, but it is as well to check first. For example, if you are on pills for your blood pressure, it may fall even more with the exercises. (In fact it may eventually be possible for your GP to reduce or even stop your medication for high blood pressure.)

BUT DO NOT STOP ANY MEDICATION WITHOUT CONSULTING YOUR GP.

4 The exercises can be a very big help for people reducing or trying to come off tranquillizers. But, we repeat, do not stop or reduce your medication without your GP's agreement and

advice. It is nearly always best to reduce tranquillizers SLOWLY, and ALWAYS under medical supervision.
5 The exercises are the best way we know for helping you to sleep and much better than sleeping pills, which may affect your essential dream sleep, affect your judgement next morning and become addictive.

We used this in a recent counselling case. John's wife had left him about three months before he came to see us. He had become very anxious, had constant headaches, was losing a lot of weight, and his state of mind and his health were now affecting his work. We found that, amongst other things, he had slept very little for three months and so was permanently tired. We agreed to support and counsel him but it was obvious that he was in no fit state to take in what we were saying. So as a first step, we started him off on the relaxation exercises. After only two nights, he was sleeping all through the night. After one week the headaches had gone and he was beginning to feel better and to think more clearly.

This gave him, and us, the initial breakthrough, and made it possible to embark on a few weeks of counselling to help him put his life and work together again.

Preparation for the exercises

1 You should practise the exercises for five minutes three times a day, with a fourth time in bed at night if you want to use them to get to sleep.
2 You need a quiet place where you will be undisturbed. You may need to take the phone off the hook.
3 Sit in a comfortable chair with your head either supported at the back or allowed to fall forward. Rest your hands gently on your thighs Or you can do the exercises lying on your back on a couch or bed with your arms by your sides.
4 Take off your glasses if you wear them, loosen any tight clothes and kick off your shoes. This will give your brain the message that you are relaxing.

5 *Relax as far as you can;* don't set yourself targets. Some people find it very difficult to relax: the harder they try, the more tense they become. SO DO NOT TRY TO RELAX. JUST FOLLOW THE INSTRUCTIONS AND LET THE RELAXATION COME. IT WILL HAPPEN BY ITSELF.

Remember, you are not practising the exercises in order to relax or sleep BUT ONLY to become good at the technique.

6 Read through the exercise notes carefully and then practise the exercises with your eyes closed in order to cut out distractions.

The relaxation exercises

1 Having closed your eyes, imagine that your arms and legs are heavy, DO NOT TRY TOO HARD but just become aware of the weight of your arms and legs. Say into yourself several times:

'My arms and legs are heavy.'

DO NOT TRY TO MAKE THEM HEAVY.

2 Imagine that your arms and legs are warm. Feel the warmth flowing down your arms from the shoulders, down the arms into your fingers – and similarly down your legs into your feet and toes. Say into yourself several times:

'My arms and legs are warm.'

DO NOT TRY TO MAKE THEM WARM.

3 And then let your breathing deepen. DO NOT PURPOSELY TAKE BIG DEEP BREATHS – LET IT HAPPEN. Say into yourself several times slowly:

'My breathing is deep and regular.'

4 Before you finish, say several times into yourself slowly:

'My neck and shoulders are heavy.'

and repeat to yourself a phrase like:

> 'The Lord is my shepherd' *or*
> 'Be still and know that I am God' *or*
> one of your favourite promises from God *or*
> simply something like 'God really loves me' *or*
> 'I am at peace with God' *or*
> 'I am perfectly relaxed' *or*
> 'God has everything in hand.'

You can say these words either silently or aloud.

5 Sit or lie with your eyes closed for a few minutes if you want to and enjoy the relaxation.

6 It is important to finish this exercise properly. Before you open your eyes and get up –
   – clench both fists tightly;
   – bend your arms at the elbow and tense your arm muscles;
   – stretch your hands above your head;
   – take a deep breath.
   OPEN YOUR EYES.
   GET UP SLOWLY.

Note – the only time you need not go into this closing routine is when you are doing the exercises last thing at night in bed – but in any case you will almost always be asleep before you finish them. Do not try to stay awake to go through the closing routine!

If you do waken up during the night, start the exercises again and you will soon go back to sleep (but don't use the closing routine, of course).

This may all sound very complicated just at this moment, but you will very soon master the technique and be able to remember it.

Postscript

1 You don't have to believe in the exercises. All you have to do is DO THEM. They will have their own effects.
2 Don't try to relax – instead, practise and become good at the exercises.
3 Do them regularly – three times per day.
4 Why not run an experiment with yourself? Decide you are going to do the exercises every day until the end of the course, and then evaluate their worth and the results on yourself. You can then decide whether the benefit has been such that you want to continue to do them regularly after that.

Action this day

START PRACTISING THE RELAXATION EXERCISES.

Thoughts for today

• Be still, and know that I am God. (Psalm 46:10)
• 'In repentance and rest is your salvation, in quietness and trust is your strength.' (Isaiah 30:15)

*

SALT (STRESS AND LIFE TRUST) has produced a teaching tape giving more details about the background and uses of this technique and how to practise it. It is obtainable from SALT, The Istana, Freezeland Lane, Bexhill on Sea, East Sussex, TN39 5JD (0424 219133).

Day 2

Fitness – exercise

People who are physically fit are less vulnerable to pressures. They can take things on and deal with them more easily; are not so easily fatigued and have more energy; are not so likely to become anxious or depressed; have a better self-image; and recover from setbacks more quickly.

SO, IT IS IMPORTANT TO BECOME AND STAY AS FIT AS POSSIBLE.

Fitness is not just the absence of disease or illness but something much more positive.

We know from medical research that a number of major factors determine how fit we are or how we can become fitter, and we are going to deal with these briefly in the first few days of the course.

If you are already quite fit – good, you can use these days to become even fitter. If you know you are not very fit, then do not despair. You can become fitter than you are quite quickly and easily.

THE MOST IMPORTANT THING IS TO MAKE A START!

If you follow the guidelines then every day you will become a little fitter. But DO NOT try or expect to become an Olympic champion in a week, or even by the end of the course for that matter! In any case, it is neither necessary nor even desirable to become super-fit.

And remember – you are never too old or too young to become fitter, so do not let age put you off either.

Exercise

Exercise can improve our physical and mental health. Apart from the obvious ways of helping – like being good for our hearts and lungs and muscles – exercise

RELEASES BENEFICIAL CHEMICALS

in our bodies.

When we exercise, and afterwards, we feel better and can cope with problems more easily. At the same time exercise calms us down. It is a wonderful natural tranquillizer and keeps us from becoming depressed. In fact, in one study of depressed patients, exercise improved them so much that many were able to reduce their medication.

If you already get regular brisk exercise, brisk enough to get you a little out of breath, for at least thirty–forty minutes, three or four times a week, then carry on.

If you do not get regular brisk exercise, a few words of advice.

a) *Before you start*, see your own GP for advice and if necessary for a check-up. This is particularly important if you are on medication or have any medical condition or if you are over forty.

b) *Start slowly* – no more than five minutes per day to begin with, increasing gradually to thirty–forty minutes.

c) *Do it regularly* – three or four times every week.

d) *Stop* if you get any pain anywhere, or if you get unduly out of breath – get medical advice before you continue or start again.

e) *Enjoy it.* Try to find a way of exercising that you enjoy. Like most things, you will enjoy it more as you get used to it and do it regularly. If you had a favourite exercise, like swimming, cycling, golf, tennis or dancing, consider taking it up again. If it is years since you did it, do prepare and start slowly. If you have never indulged in such a sport or exercise, consider taking one up. If you have no great love of sport, then walking – as long as your legs and feet are healthy – is an excellent form of exercise, especially if you swing your arms as you walk.

If you have mobility problems with, for example, arthritis of the knees, hips, ankles or back, then swimming may be better for you. Exercise is also possible in a sitting position.

A small start, even walking short distances, is good. Plan to leave your car a little bit further from the station, shops, school or work, every day, and walk the rest of the way. Go out for a walk at lunchtime instead of sitting in the office. Exercise your body rather than your tongue or your mind sometimes. Walk up stairs at work or in the shops instead of taking the lift or escalator.

THE IMPORTANT THING IS TO MAKE A START

– it will soon become a good habit.

If you want something more structured, start with a short walk each day, *gradually* increasing the distance and the speed and the hills. Or you may prefer to invest in an exercise bicycle, which is certainly easier on dark, wet winter nights.

Or if you want something even more formal, consider joining a fitness club – but do get advice from the experts before you go on the apparatus.

THE IMPORTANT THING IS TO MAKE A START

– it will soon become a good habit and you will come to like it, even enjoy it. Believe it or not, you will begin to miss it when you don't have your exercise period.

It is often easier to start something and get into it if you have company. See if you can persuade a friend or member of the family to start with you. Mutual encouragement can be a great help, especially in the early days.

Many companies have seen the sense of providing exercise facilities at work: it keeps individuals fit, cuts down stress levels and sickness absence and may increase productivity. Churches could consider putting in an exercise room. Many leaders would benefit from regular exercise just as much as their church members do. I know of some fellowships where this facility has helped the physical, mental and spiritual health of members, brought families together and been the initial contact for those outside the church. (A good investment for any church. Think about it, church leaders).

Prayer

Dear Heavenly Father,
  Thank you for the health I have and the body you have given me. Please forgive me for not looking after my body more. I want to appreciate just how wonderfully I have been made.
  I want to give you not only my spirit and my soul, but my body also, for you to use in any way you choose. I mean to look after my body more and to exercise enough to keep me as fit as possible. In Jesus's name, Amen.

Action this day

1 Arrange a check-up with your GP prior to starting to exercise more — especially if you are on medication, have health problems or are over forty.
2 Decide where you can walk daily instead of driving, taking a taxi, a lift or an escalator.
3 Plan to start some regular exercise either today or after a check-up.
4 REMEMBER – START

  – START SLOWLY – BUT START NOW.

Thoughts for today

- Do you not know that your body is a temple of the Holy Spirit, who is in you, whom you have received from God? You are not your own; you were brought at a price. Therefore honour God with your body. (1 Corinthians 6:19, 20)

- Therefore, I urge you, brothers, in view of God's mercy, to offer your bodies as living sacrifices, holy and pleasing to God – this is your spiritual act of worship. (Romans 12:1)
- For physical training is of some value . . . (1 Timothy 4:8)

HAVE YOU PRACTISED YOUR RELAXATION EXERCISES TODAY? THEY WILL ONLY HELP IF YOU DO THEM!

We saw yesterday that physical fitness helps us to deal with pressures, and we dealt with the first important factor in becoming and staying fit – EXERCISE.

Today we deal with the second – WEIGHT. It is not a good thing, or necessary, to become preoccupied by our weight. In fact it can be dangerous if it gets a hold of us, and can lead to eating disorders. On the other hand, to ignore it altogether is not wise and may lead to health problems.

There is nothing wrong with being on the thin side as long as we are eating wisely and are otherwise healthy. Some people, however, become very conscious of being slim, often because someone has referred to them as being 'skinny', or 'bony' or 'all angles', and they try desperately to put on weight. They should realize that generally speaking it is much healthier to be slim than to be overweight. The chances are that the remarks about their being thin were made either out of ignorance or from a certain envy by those who are, or are tending to be, overweight.

On the other hand, if you are losing a good deal of weight and your clothes are becoming loose then it is as well to have a check-up to exclude a medical cause which may need treatment.

Being grossly overweight or steadily putting on a lot of weight makes it difficult for our body to function effectively.

Imagine carrying one, two or even three stones of potatoes around everywhere you go. You wouldn't be surprised to get out of breath and tire easily, or find that you were putting a strain on parts of your body. If we are considerably overweight then it stands to reason that this will tire us out, putting a strain on our heart and lungs and our blood pressure may go up in order to cope. It is bound, also, to put a strain on our backs, hips, knees, ankles and feet when we walk or climb – possibly producing the early wear and tear of arthritis. Chronic conditions and pain can get us down, and it is then more difficult to cope with pressures.

But being fit is not just about the absence of disease, and being reasonably trim makes us feel better, with more energy, less puffing and panting, and with a better outlook on life, a better self-image – all helping us to deal with pressures.

IT IS WISE THEREFORE TO KEEP OR ATTAIN A REASONABLE WEIGHT.

If you are grossly overweight, then it isn't really necessary to weigh yourself to know. You may need professional help first of all to find out whether there is a medical, or perhaps glandular, problem, and then with treatment and a suitable diet; Or there may be some deep-seated emotional reason which has to be uncovered and dealt with before your eating habits normalize and you can lose weight, and you may need help with a special diet.

For most of us, however, there is no serious cause underlying our weight gain. It is usually insidious, and especially in middle age, we begin to spread. As our clothes get tighter and we begin to notice the tell-tale signs in the mirror, we blame it first on our posture, then on clothes shrinking in the wash, and as we capitulate to larger sizes we soften the blow by telling ourselves that these European sizes are different and that this or that article of clothing is a 'small fitting'. But it is very important, if you want to stay fit or get fitter, that

YOU DO NOT LET YOUR WEIGHT GET OUT OF HAND.

The main cause of being overweight is OVEREATING.

We see many people who are overweight, and invariably they claim that they eat very little. The bad news, if this is true, is that they are still eating too much – for them. There is no doubt that some people seem to be able to eat and eat and burn it up and not put on weight, while others only have to look at a cream cake and they put on weight. If you are one of these, then it is really hard on you, but the answer is still almost certainly that you must eat less.

Regular exercise, which we dealt with yesterday, will help to keep weight down but it is not a very efficient way of losing weight. A director of a company Bill was medical officer for was a gourmet and really enjoyed his food. He had a season ticket for a large and famous restaurant on the sea front. Bill watched as he steadily put on weight, and at the first opportunity checked his blood pressure, which was also creeping up.

'You really must watch your weight,' Bill said. 'Right. I'll start exercising,' was his reply. 'That would be good for you, but do you know that you would have to walk to London to burn off what you are likely to take in, in one of your business lunches?' Bill told him. 'The only way really is fewer visits to the restaurants, fewer courses or smaller helpings.'

A strict diet appeals to some. (We wonder how many books have been written about special diets? We are sure we could make a lot of money from a 'Waist Disposal Clinic'!) But one problem is that few people can stick to a diet for long, let alone permanently. So the weight comes off – and the weight goes on when the diet stops.

We heard of one man who lost 280 pounds over a few years. How? Simple. He would go on a diet, lose a few stones, put them back on, lose a few more again and so on. He lost a lot of weight over a period but in the end never weighed any less.

Another problem with diets is that the body seems to adjust to the new diet so that it becomes more and more difficult to lose weight.

It is better to be careful if your weight starts to go up, and at that stage cut down slowly on the intake.

For many of us strategies to help us avoid eating so much are better than a diet. In Bill's book *Designer Living*, he suggests a few: such as buying smaller plates, going to the supermarket on a full stomach, not having weight-disastrous snacks in the house – a bowl of fruit is much better.

For some of us, losing weight or keeping it within bounds may seem like a daunting task, but it is important

TO MAKE A START.

Like starting to exercise, cutting down your food intake will become a habit. But

DON'T GET NEUROTIC ABOUT IT

– either your intake or your weight. The first important thing is that you do not get any fatter or eat more; and secondly – if you are already too heavy or are eating too much, that the trend over a period is downwards.

DO NOT FEEL GUILTY ABOUT THE ODD RELAPSE OR BLIP

– because you have been out for a meal or enjoyed a sticky bun. In fact it is quite a good plan occasionally to allow yourself a treat.

Feeling guilty or trying too hard will increase the tension, making it more likely that you will not succeed.

One helpful tip is not to make your standard of 'success' actually losing weight, but rather cutting down on what you eat. You do have control over what you put in your mouth, but you do not have direct control over how fast you lose weight. Otherwise you will regularly feel defeated if your weight fluctuates (which it will do) and then you may give in by eating too much in consolation.

If you do break your limits of eating (which you will sometimes do) you can always start again the next day, and you can have regular 'successes' which will build your confidence and encourage you to continue. Let the weight loss take care of itself.

Do not weigh yourself more than once a week so that you can avoid being drawn into the 'weight loss trap'. Treat any weight loss as an item of interest rather than a personal victory or measure of your personal worth (which is very much behind the struggles we usually have in our society – leading to neurotic preoccupation with how we look).

Prayer

Dear Father God,

You have given me the body I have but I acknowledge that it is my duty to look after it. I can see that in your eyes there may be little difference between addiction to drugs or alcohol, or tobacco or food.

I ask for your help now as I seek to acquire/maintain a reasonable food intake.

Show me what strategies I should adopt to achieve this and please give me your power to keep to them. Amen.

Action this day

1 IF you are grossly overweight – arrange today to see your GP or dietician.
2 IF you have been losing weight recently (and have not been on a diet) – arrange to see your GP today for a check-up.
3 IF you are *somewhat* overweight, WORK OUT 3 STRATEGIES for eating less and START ON THEM TODAY.
4 IF your weight is *average* – work out 3 strategies for keeping it as it is and START ON THEM TODAY.

WEIGH YOURSELF TODAY – AND AGAIN AT THE END OF THE COURSE.

DON'T MAKE WEIGHT LOSS YOUR CRITERION OF SUCCESS. MAKE KEEPING TO YOUR EATING STRATEGIES YOUR SUCCESS – ON A DAILY BASIS.

Remember, success builds on success!

Thoughts for today

- Do you not know that your body is a temple of the Holy Spirit?
  (1 Corinthians 6:19)
- – and put a knife to your throat if you are given to gluttony.
  (Proverbs 23:2)

HAVE YOU PLANNED OR STARTED YOUR EXERCISE
PROGRAMME? DONE YOUR RELAXATION EXERCISES
TODAY?

Day 4

Fitness – healthy eating

Carrot addiction

Yes, you can become addicted to carrots. *The British Journal of Addiction* reported in 1992 about three patients who became addicted to them, one of whom had managed to give up smoking by switching to carrots. When they could not get their carrots, the patients became nervous and irritable and craved for them!

A healthy diet

Healthy eating can keep us healthy and fit, giving us a zest for life and protecting us from pressures.

We saw yesterday that it is not wise to become obsessed by weight. The same applies to diet, unless there is some special diet we have to keep to because of a medical condition. Special fad diets can be expensive and are seldom necessary. Extra vitamins and minerals, too, are only necessary in specific or exceptional circumstances. However, it is important that we pay some attention to what we eat.

Eating too little can result in starvation or malnutrition. A diet short in essentials can cause deficiency diseases. If we eat a normal 'balanced' diet and do not have to exclude certain foods because of specific allergies or other medical reasons, then we are probably getting enough of the nutrients essential for healthy living.

Current medical and health research, however, recommends that we cut down on certain foods.

Too much animal fat may lead to artery and heart problems.

Was God being literal when He said, 'This is a lasting ordinance for the generations to come, wherever you live; you must not eat any fat – or blood' (Leviticus 3:17), and again in Leviticus 7:23 where He says, 'Do not eat any of the fat of cattle, sheep or goats'?

Dairy products like strong cheeses, butter and cream contain fats and cholesterol and are bad news for our hearts and blood vessels, so reduce them or use substitutes where possible. We need the calcium in milk for our bones and teeth – but skimmed milk is better than full cream.

Too many sweet things – sugar, sweets, biscuits, cakes – are not good for us.

Avoid excess salt, especially if you have a tendency to high blood pressure.

Try to eat more fish, lean meat (especially white meat like chicken) and get plenty of vegetables, fruit and roughage, like bran or brown bread. Soup with a brown bread salad sandwich with tuna fish or salmon makes a good and satisfying lunch. Eskimos suffer less from heart conditions than we do. It is thought that this is because of the protection they get from a special constituent in the oil of the fish they eat; so our diet should contain fish like pilchards, sardines and mackerel.

As with so many things, just thinking of what we should be doing and then not doing it – in this case, what we should be eating or not eating – will not do us any good.

BUT, IT IS IMPORTANT TO BEGIN.

You will be surprised how quickly a healthier diet becomes a habit. If you persevere without sugar in tea or coffee, and without added salt in main meals you will soon begin to prefer things without added sugar or added salt.

In our home we only use skimmed milk now. Occasionally when we eat out or with friends we find that we actually don't like full cream milk on the cereals, or in tea or coffee – it tastes too creamy and rich. The same applies to many other items once you have made a start.

Stimulants such as strong tea, coffee or cola can keep you awake and help you to perform better, but be careful you don't come to rely on them for energy. Too much, too often, can be bad for your health and you can become addicted.

A good general guide about diet is still

MODERATION IN ALL THINGS.

Prayer

Dear Father,

I do appreciate the health you give me. I want to be as healthy and fit as I can be. I realize that what I eat is important, especially if I want to be able to deal with whatever pressures come to me.

I intend, with your help, to keep to a balanced diet.

In Jesus's name, Amen.

Action this day

1 Make a start on healthy eating today.
2 Take a list of healthy foods on your next visit to the supermarket – and stick to it.

Thoughts for today

• If you listen carefully to the voice of the Lord your God and do what is right in His eyes, if you pay attention to His commands and keep all His decrees, I will not bring on you any of the diseases I brought on the Egyptians, for I am the Lord, who heals you. (Exodus 15:26)

HAVE YOU DONE YOUR RELAXATION EXERCISES TODAY?
DON'T FORGET YOUR REGULAR EXERCISE TODAY.
THINK ABOUT WHAT YOU ARE EATING. THINK SLIM.

Day 5

The value of support

There are few, if any, of us who do not face pressures, sometimes bigger, sometimes smaller, at one period or another of our life.

You may be facing problems and pressures at this time.

It may be pressure at work, a new job, new methods, more demands, a difficult boss, unco-operative colleagues, unfair criticism, fear of redundancy or early retirement, anxieties about the future.

It may be pressure in the family – broken sleep with small babies, never-ending piles of washing and ironing, demands of toddlers and the 'terrible twos'; or it may be anxieties about your children at school – under-achieving, bullying, or rebellious teenagers; a difficult spouse, or parents who just do not understand; loss of a loved one through death, separation or divorce; chronic ill health, or serious illness; physical, mental or sexual abuse; or it may be pressures in the home – difficulties in making ends meet, paying the bills, debt, mortgage, repossession; or perhaps you are facing the frustration and helplessness of redundancy, unemployment or business failure; or pressures in the church – disagreements, division, splits, lack of funds.

The list seems endlessly depressing and may not even end there for you, as you can add on your own specific problems.

BUT NOW FOR SOME GOOD NEWS.

Many studies have shown that THOSE WHO GET SUPPORT WHEN THEY ARE UNDER PRESSURE ARE LESS VULNER-ABLE. They are less likely to become and stay anxious, and to develop stress-related conditions. On the other hand, those who do not get support are more vulnerable and more likely to go under.

Traditional Italian communities in the USA – with extended family support networks – have low rates of heart attacks, despite high fat diets, smoking and lack of exercise (though this of course does not negate the need for a good diet and exercise, as we have seen over the past few days).

Support has been shown, too, to help recovery after a heart attack.

Love and TLC – Tender Loving Care – are important parts of support. In an Israeli study, love and support from wives helped to prevent men developing angina, even when they had high blood cholesterol levels and high blood pressure.

Some years ago, a trial was carried out on rabbits to test the effect of a high cholesterol diet. The rabbits were divided into two groups. One group was fed a normal diet and the other a diet high in fats and cholesterol.

At the end of the study, as expected, the hearts of the rabbits fed the normal diet were in good shape, while those fed the high fat diet had furred-up arteries with badly affected hearts. All, that is, except for one small sub-group, who were fed the high fat diet but showed no damage to arteries or hearts. Consternation in the lab! How could this be? Records were checked and double checked, in case there had been some mistake in the diet administration. No, everything was in order. There had been no mistakes. The only thing that came to light was that this small group had been looked after by a soft-hearted young lab technician who, every night before she went home, took her rabbits out of their cages and cuddled and stroked them. This TLC was thought to have protected the rabbits' arteries and hearts against the high fat diet!

It has been estimated that we all need ten–twelve hugs a day – to help our cholesterol levels. A few years ago there was a National Hugging Day, with the slogan, 'A hug a day keeps the doctor away.' It could bear much repeating!

English people are often not very touch- or hugging-orientated, but it can be learned and become a habit. We know of one family where the mother had learned about the benefits of hugging. Unfortunately they were not a hugging family and there was a great deal of embarrassment to overcome. However, she determined to do what she could to improve their health. She would take up a position at the door whenever any member of the family was going out and demand a hug. She kept this up for a month and slowly, would you believe, all began to expect it and indeed to look for it and enjoy it once the initial awkwardness wore off. It had become a really good habit.

God has instructed us to love one another and bear one another's burdens, because He knows that sometimes life will be difficult and we all need support from others.

Jesus's story of the Good Samaritan is an encouragement for us all to love those in need. But there is another side to the coin: without support and help, what would have happened to the traveller? Had it not been for the Good Samaritan it is unlikely that he would have survived.

If you are in a position to give help to someone today, then please give it.

The support people need may vary from time to time – an encouraging word, a hand on the shoulder, a friendly smile, a cup of tea, a listening ear, a shoulder to cry on, a helping hand with the children or the housework or the shopping or the gardening; a gift in kind or money; common-sense advice; advice from experience; expert advice; encouragement from a Bible story or passage or text; or professional medical or pastoral counselling; or the need may just be for someone to be there.

However, it is essential that any support offered should be non-judgemental, unconditional, the no-strings-attached kind of support, otherwise it will become a burden and curse to the person in need, rather than a blessing. The essence of support is that we find out what the other person is needing from us before we assume that we know what they need. Self-righteous support is worse than none at all, and we should not do it to bolster our own sense of self worth.

DO NOT UNDERESTIMATE THE PROFOUND EFFECT YOUR SUPPORT MAY HAVE ON OTHERS

– it may even be life-saving, and the effect may be far beyond the cost to you.

If YOU have problems at this time or see them coming START THINKING ABOUT SUPPORT NOW – if possible before the pressures get out of hand. (Tomorrow we will look at some of the possible sources of support.)

If you have no specific pressures at present then now is the time to start building up a mutual support network, so that it is in place and readily available at any time it may be needed.

Prayer

My Heavenly Father,

You have told us to support and love one another. Please help me to give support to those that I know, or will meet today, who need it. Guide me about the form this support should take.

You know that I myself need support too. I ask that you will lead me to the support I need or send just the kind and amount that I need today.

I know that you love me, and I trust you for the support I need. For Jesus's sake, Amen.

Action this day

1 If there are no drastic pressures on you at this time:
   a) resolve slowly to build up a network of support for use in the future when you will need it;
   b) speak to someone today who needs support, and offer what you can.
2 If you are in the midst of pressures, resolve today to seek out appropriate support.

Thoughts for today

- Jesus said, 'A new command I give you: Love one another. As I have loved you, so you must love one another. All men will know that you are my disciples if you love one another.' (John 13:34, 35)
- Carry each other's burdens, and in this way you will fulfil the law of Christ. (Galatians 6:2)

Don't forget:

RELAXATION EXERCISES! EXERCISE! HEALTHY EATING!

Sources of support

We saw yesterday that support, care and love are very big factors in helping us to cope with pressures.

We suggested that you give support wherever and whenever you can; that if you are in the midst of pressures you should look for support *now*; and if life is reasonably peaceful at the moment, you should start building up a network of support for use when it is needed.

But where to look for support?

Here are a few suggestions. Some may be relevant to your situation or they may spark off other ideas in your mind.

God said, 'It is not good for the man [Adam] to be alone. I will make a helper suitable for him [Eve].'

If your husband, wife or family is supportive and understanding, then they will probably be the nearest source of possible support. If you have not told your spouse or members of your family about your fears or problems, then think about doing this today and ask for their help.

However, it may be that your family is part of the problem, or they may be too close to your problem to be able to help; or you may not have any immediate family. What about close friends or neighbours?

Jesus said, 'Love your neighbour as yourself.' Are there any you can trust, to listen and not to pass it on? If you have, then consider sharing with one of them. If you don't have caring friends you can rely on, then it is perhaps time to make contacts who can become friends and sources of support in the future.

If you work, a starting point for finding support may be your boss, or the personnel or welfare department, or the occupational health nurse or doctor, or a caring colleague. But we can understand if you do not want others at work to learn about your problems. This is why a number of companies are introducing EAPs (Employee Assistance Programmes). Employees can ring up an independent service, retained by the company but not part of it, for completely impartial and confidential advice on any subject, or for counselling. The company is never provided with details or names of those who use the service, so that employees can feel confident that their problems will not be known within the company.

The Citizens' Advice Bureau can often give practical advice for you to act on, or they may be able to put you in touch with other expert advice or with voluntary organizations who specialize in the area giving you problems.

Your church is or should be your extended family. Members of it, after all, are your brothers and sisters in Christ. So you should be able to go to other members or leaders for love and support, knowing that you will not be judged, or misunderstood, or rejected or spurned. It is wonderful to be a member of such a loving church or house group. There are many around nowadays and well worth looking for.

It is sad but perhaps understandable, however, that, for a variety of reasons, Christians often prefer to seek support outside their own local church. They don't want their leaders, friends and fellow members to know about their problems. They feel that they would not be able to be entirely open with people they know. Sometimes there is a possibility, too, that things will not be absolutely confidential if the 'rule' in the church is that all the leaders want to know about any counselling going on, and to share everything with each other. If you do decide to share with a leader or counsellor within the church, it is as well to know who else may have access to your problems so that you are not surprised and hurt or disappointed later.

For these and many other reasons, our own organization, SALT (Stress And Life Trust), like other counsellors and counselling organizations, often sees people from outside the immediate area and sometimes from quite far afield. Like many others you may decide to seek help or counselling outside your local church.

Your GP may be able to help you directly or put you in touch with another relevant source of help, like the social services or a voluntary organization. Or he may refer you for counselling.

If you are referred, or your company has an Employee Assistance Programme, or if you look for counselling yourself, it is important to find out something about the counsellor and type of counselling you are likely to receive. There are many schools of therapy and of counselling. Some can be actually harmful but others of great benefit. Some are at odds with Christian teaching and others not contradictory to it. Many are humanistic, and try to bolster and strengthen the individual him- or herself.

There are Christian counsellors. However, it is important to distinguish between Christian counselling and counselling from a Christian who may be trained in and use any of the different forms of psychotherapy, or may not be trained at all.

You should be able to depend on Christian counselling from a trained Christian counsellor. The recently formed Association of Christian Counsellors has a register of names and addresses. Perhaps in the future we may have church EAPs.

Irrespective of where you decide to turn to for help and support, it is important that you

DO NOT DELAY.

Men are often so macho that they think they don't need support, seeing it as a sign of weakness.

Those in the caring professions are another group who feel that they do not or should not need support – doctors, nurses, social workers, teachers, clergy and church leaders. We are the ones who give support. We are not supposed to need it. What will people think if we need support? But

WE ALL NEED SUPPORT because WE ARE ALL HUMAN.

Prayer

Heavenly Father,
I admit that often I need help and support and you know this.
Please guide me to an appropriate source of help or advice or
Christian counselling.
Please show me where and when I should be offering help
and support. For Jesus's sake, Amen.

Action this day

1 Consider potential sources of support.
2 Check them out, regarding the help they can give.
3 Then seek support from the most appropriate source TODAY
   – if you are in the midst of problems.

Thoughts for today

- And in the church God has appointed first of all apostles,
  second prophets, third teachers, then workers of miracles, also
  those having gifts of healing, those able to help others, those
  with gifts of administration, and those speaking in different
  kinds of tongues. (1 Corinthians 12:28)

ACC – The Association of Christian Counsellors
Kings House
175 Wokingham Road
READING
Bekshire RG6 1LT
Tel. 0734 662207

Decisions, choices, priorities

Not making decisions or choices when they are required can lead to unexpected things just happening to us, and we may end up stressed.

So it is good to make decisions. But choosing between conflicting priorities can itself be stressful for us. And if we make wrong choices or priorities, the consequences can lead to stress for us.

How do we pick our way through this minefield? Let us take a closer look at this important subject of decisions, choices and priorities.

All through life, at every stage and every day, in fact almost all the time – we have to make decisions.

We are not always aware that most, if not all, of these decisions involve a choice or choices. Almost everything we do involves us in a choice. Did you realize that today you will have to make a very big number – perhaps hundreds – of choices?

The very fact of doing something means that we have chosen to do it rather than not doing it. We have chosen to do it now rather than later. We have chosen to do it rather than something else at this particular time. We have chosen to devote time, energy, resources, attention, care, perhaps money to it, rather than to other things. We have also chosen how we are going to do it.

Even when we feel that we *have* to do something or are being forced to do it in a certain way, the ultimate choice is ours as to whether we do it or not, and when, and how. These choices, of course, may entail consequences. If we choose not to do something our boss has asked us to do, or to do it at a different time or in a different way from what he or she required, then we may earn disapproval, affect our promotion, our salary or even our job itself. But in the end, we do have the choice, albeit sometimes a difficult one.

However, even when we have as much freedom as possible we still have to make choices.

We wonder how many choices you made yesterday without even realizing you were making them? If you are intrigued by this, why not start counting all the choices you make during the rest of today.

The main reason that so many choices are necessary at every turn, in every aspect of our lives, is that resources of every kind are not infinite. All are limited.

Wealth and money are limited. So politicians have to choose how much will be spent on defence, or hospitals or schools. Health service chiefs have to choose how much will go on kidney dialysis or GPs or care of the mentally ill or of old people. We have to choose whether we spend money on a new car, or a new lawnmower, or on repairing the old, or on a new suit or dress or a holiday.

WE HAVE TO CHOOSE.

Our time is limited. So we have to choose how we will spend Sunday morning: washing the car, or mowing the lawn, or reading the papers, or taking the children to the park, or helping our wife or husband in the house, or visiting ageing parents or children, or going to church.

WE HAVE TO CHOOSE.

Our capacity for giving care, love and attention is limited. This evening, will we choose to devote it to ourselves or to others – enjoying a night in the pub or with friends, or a good book, or working in our study, or doing the ironing, or spending time sitting with our wife or husband, or reading or playing with our children, or caring for others through charity work, the church or the rotary club or fund raising?

WE HAVE TO CHOOSE.

As well as having to choose what we will do or not do and how we will do it, we often have to choose what will be done first or what will get more money, time, attention than other things – in other words

WE HAVE TO CHOOSE PRIORITIES.

This will always imply that the lowest priorities may suffer and get fewer resources, or if they run out – perhaps none at all. Unfortunately, very often

WE DO NOT MAKE CONSCIOUS, INFORMED CHOICES.

We may allow them to be made for us: 'It needs to be done.' We may make them to protect ourselves: 'If I don't do it . . . will be angry'; or to satisfy demands being made on us, to quieten the clamour for our attention or resources: 'If I do this they will get off my back'; or because of feelings of guilt or because of emotional blackmail: 'I can do without hassle'.

Sometimes we may even feel like opting out of making choices. We busy ourselves with whatever is to hand, or nearest or easiest. The day passes and we comfort ourselves with the fact that we have never been idle.

But we still made a choice when we chose to opt out.

The importance of all of this is that as far as and as often as possible we should

BE AWARE WHEN WE ARE MAKING CHOICES

and then CHOOSE WITH OUR EYES WIDE OPEN.

Choosing priority for things with immediate consequences is fairly easy. If we do not drop everything to turn the cooker down NOW – the saucepan will boil over or the contents be burned.

Even with medium-term things it is fairly easy to assess and then prioritize time and resources. If we do not put money and time aside to pay the phone bill next week, then, in a few weeks, it will be cut off.

In the longer term, if we do not plan to paint the windows some time this year, then in a few years they may rot and will need to be replaced.

Similarly with our health. If we do not arrange things so that we get enough sleep tonight, then tomorrow we may fall asleep at work, or at the wheel of the car. If we do not choose to get enough sleep over a period we may become irritable, find it difficult to concentrate and make poor decisions and judgements. If we constantly choose to do without adequate sleep and recuperation we may begin to suffer from the effects of stress.

WHAT ABOUT THE REALLY BIG THINGS IN OUR LIFE?

As with so many other things, it is relatively easy to choose immediate priorities. If your child falls and hurts himself or herself, We expect you would drop most things to comfort and stop the bleeding. If your mother or father falls seriously ill, the shopping trip with your wife or husband waits while you visit your parents. If your job requires an urgent visit or an extra Saturday morning's work – the golf match has to be postponed or cancelled.

BUT WHAT ABOUT THE MEDIUM AND LONGER TERM?

At the end of the day who and what is more important to you – your job, your wife, children, parents or church, the Rotary Club, yourself or your future, God Himself?

Most of us could probably, in theory at least, put them into some kind of order of importance, but the problem really is that few of us stop to think or work it out until it is too late.

When there are no emergencies how does the attention, care, time and energy you give to them day in and day out reflect the relative importance of each to you?

If you believe that losing your wife or husband would be worse than losing your job, why do you always put your job first? If you do always put it first, can you really be too surprised when your wife or husband finds someone else who will put her or him first?

If you always put your children before your husband or wife, should you be too surprised if they yearn for someone who will put them first?

How often have you said something like, 'God, you are very important to me and I know that it's important to be doing your will and to spend time with you, but can you just hold on till next Sunday – and I'll be in touch with you then. Got to go now!'

CONSCIOUSLY CHOOSING AND ACTING UPON OUR CHOICE OF WHO AND WHAT MEANS MOST TO US IS CRUCIALLY IMPORTANT

– for our long term peace of mind.

A big source of stress in many of our lives is when there is a conflict between priorities. In an emergency it's relatively easy, but on a day-to-day basis when there is a conflict, a competition for you, do you put the one that means most to you first?

In any case, who or what should come first in our lives? How do we choose? Having chosen, how do we know that intrinsically this is the best choice? Do we base it on expediency, or on our feelings, or what?

We may have decided that our wife is more important than our job. How much do we worry, however, that our job may be at risk, when we decide to spend weekends with our wife or husband and family, rather than working flat out every Saturday and Sunday too?

How much do we fret when our ageing parents demand visits every Saturday, when we wonder if we should be spending more time with our children and wife or husband?

The answers, we believe, have been given to us by God. These are not rigid or inflexible, especially in times of emergency, but they are the general guidelines. God made us and knows how we function best, in terms of our relationships, our work, our lives and our world. This includes our priorities. If we believe this, then we can follow His guidelines without fretting too much, knowing that this is more important than the pressures being put on us by others or how we feel from day to day.

God's order of priorities for us, we believe, is to put HIM first in all things, including spending time with Him, which may be different from being busy with Christian and church work.

If we are married, our spouse should come next – not our job, or our children, or our church, or religious activities.

Then our children are next in line, as they are dependent upon us for care and protection. Then parents and family – even if they are not Christians.

Next our job, then our church and other good works, and lastly our own desires and comfort. (It is important that we have time for ourselves, as we have seen in the section on FITNESS and as we will deal with in LIFESTYLE on a later day.)

So, if and when there is conflict of interest or of demands on us, we can fall back, with confidence, on this order. This can give us much peace of mind and free us from continuing stress.

Prayer

Heavenly Father,

Thank you for giving us in the Bible so much guidance about how we should live.

Please forgive me for not actively choosing my priorities and for getting them wrong. With your help, I want to get these right in your sight. Please help me to do this with love and sensitivity, and to trust that even when there may be conflict you know best and will honour my decisions and actions in keeping to your order. In Jesus's name, Amen.

Action this day

1 Review the importance people and areas in your life.
2 List them in the order God sees them.
3 Resolve to observe this order in the normal course of events, knowing that in emergencies and special circumstances it may have to be amended FOR A TIME.

Thoughts for today

- God said, 'You shall have no other gods before me.' (Exodus 20:3)
- Jesus said, 'But seek first His kingdom, and His righteousness, and all these things will be given to you as well.' (Matthew 6:33)

Lifestyle (1)
A balanced day

All work and no play makes Jack a dull boy, and more vulnerable to pressures.

A balanced lifestyle, on the other hand, makes us less vulnerable to pressures.

A full life is good and preferable to boredom and having time hang heavily on our hands. However, when everything is a continual mad rush with no time to draw breath we can develop.

HURRY SICKNESS

and we are then an easy prey to pressures when they come –

A BALANCE IS NEEDED.

For some, such as a single parent or a working mother with young children, it is difficult to achieve a balance between doing and relaxing. Others are afraid to slow down from being perpetually on the go, because it may lead to them having time to reflect on their life and its meaning.

There is a story of a fighter pilot out over the Pacific being contacted by his base, who were a bit worried about him. 'How are you and what is your position?' 'I'm fine, and I'm making a really fast time, but I'm not sure of my position or direction'!

Others are never still, not through design, but because they have taken on too much, never say 'No' and never give up any obligation once they have take it on. Eventually their schedule is absolutely choc-a-bloc. An old saying is very true:

IF YOU WANT TO GET ANYTHING DONE – ASK A BUSY PERSON!

Like so many worthwhile things in life, it is not enough to agree in theory, 'Yes, a balanced lifestyle is a good thing'. Because we know it will be good for us, not just for others, we must choose, decide and then carry through in actions.

So how do we achieve a balanced lifestyle?

Let's start with each single day. We've all been told, at some time or other, to LIVE ONE DAY AT A TIME – but what does this mean?

It does NOT mean ignoring all our yesterdays. Memories can be pleasurable. We can learn from our experiences, our failures and our successes. But it does mean not living in the past. Once we have confessed our failures and mistakes to God and have decided what we can learn from them for today and the future, we should stop feeling guilty and worrying about what has been.

GOD HAS FORGIVEN US AND FORGOTTEN AND SO SHOULD WE.

The 'Accuser of the brethren' has succeeded when we still feel guilty about things for which God has forgiven us.

Living one day at a time also does NOT mean ignoring tomorrow and the future. It is good to plan and even to spend some time dreaming about the future – our vision.

IF YOU FAIL TO PLAN, YOU ARE PLANNING TO FAIL.

Living one day at a time DOES MEAN not worrying about tomorrow or the future. Our culture is full of sayings, many of which are very helpful, like

'Smile, it may never happen.'

'Don't cross your bridges till you come to them.'

One of the busiest periods in the history of the world was the first six days when God created everything. At the end of each day God 'saw that it was good'. He did not spend time worrying about what He had not done nor what He was going to do the next day. He presumably relaxed, looked at what He had done and said 'Good'.

Personally, we have found it useful to look back over the day before sleeping at night, to thank God for the day that's gone and the opportunities it brought, to ask for forgiveness for sins of omission and commission, to seek His peace and then sleep soundly. There was a time when Bill would lie in bed and plan the next day. Even when he was not worried about what it would hold he found that by going over in his mind what he would do and how he would do it, he became alert and then found it difficult to relax and sleep. He now waits and does his 'planning' in the morning when he wakes. So he sleeps better and becomes alert in the morning as he plans the day. So –

ONE DAY AT A TIME.

Burning the midnight oil may be necessary from time to time when there are important deadlines to meet, but this should not become the rule. 'Early to bed, early to rise makes a man healthy, wealthy and wise.'

The electric light has been a wonderful invention but it has tempted us to lengthen and lengthen our working day. While not suggesting that we should always stick rigidly to an 8-hour day or the hours of daylight only, perhaps we should ponder that God's natural light gives us limited hours to work normally. People often say that despite the aggravations, they enjoyed the period of power cuts. They sat about talking more, had more rest and went to bed earlier. Some shift work is necessary but rapidly revolving shifts are often stressful.

Certainly we should normally try to get adequate hours of sleep. Sleep is necessary for recuperation of the body and the mind. We go through various stages of sleep each night – and one of them, REM (Rapid Eye Movement) sleep, is when we dream. Dreaming is good for us and probably allows the brain to resort and refile material. Do we realize how important dreaming is? A lot of important dreams are recorded in the Bible!

Some people can thrive on comparatively few hours of sleep, but eight hours per night is average. So as long as you feel refreshed, don't worry that you are getting less than average. Sleeping pills should be a last resort. They can be addictive and also can interfere with the normal sleep patterns – including REM sleep and dreaming.

If your mind is still active when you go to bed, with 'alert' chemicals circulating and bathing your brain, then sleep or certainly restful and peaceful sleep is less likely. It is a good idea to start winding down some hours before trying to sleep.

If you do have to concentrate or use your brain in the evening, especially on work you have brought home to keep up with demands on you, then stop no later than nine o'clock and give yourself time to wind down.

We see many school teachers these days suffering from the effects of stress. Their daytime problems may be complicated by not sleeping well at night. This is often associated with marking papers or preparing work for the next day, far into the night. Improvement always follows the advice to stop working at nine – no matter what.

Pacing yourself during the day is important. We are not all at our best at the same times each day. So try to find when you are most alert, and most productive and most creative, and try to arrange your day accordingly, leaving the more humdrum activities to your less able times.

Whenever possible take short breaks during the day. If you can sit down, put your feet up, close your eyes, even for a few moments, at the end of a task or in the middle of a long one, this can greatly refresh you. If you spend most of the day sitting then plan short breaks when you can walk here or there on an errand.

When morale and productivity were extremely important during the Second World War, 'Workers' Playtime', a lunchtime music and variety programme, became very popular in factories and on the radio throughout the country. With the severe pressures on us nowadays, perhaps industry should be taking a leaf out of the wartime book. Meanwhile, you can have your own short 'playtime'.

There is a great temptation to work through the lunch hour. This is not good for health or concentration or productivity, and is quite the opposite of 'Workers' Playtime'. It is much wiser to take a full lunch hour, change down gear, relax and allow the stomach to digest sandwiches or lunch.

When there is a lot on your mind, during periods of stress or worry, you can spend much of each day worrying about circumstances and what you should do about them. The worrying itself can become stressful and interfere with your normal functioning at work or at home. At times like these when worrying thoughts often come into your mind try the following strategy: reserve a special time of the day, perhaps fifteen or even thirty minutes, as

WORRY TIME

when you can give yourself totally to thinking about the problems or worries and their solutions. When thoughts come at other times, make a note of them then say to yourself: 'I will think about this during my worry period later, so I do not need to concern myself with this now.' Amazingly you will find that your mind and body will accept this and you can then get on with your normal activity unhampered at that time by incessant, distracting and debilitating worrying thoughts and anxiety.

REMEMBER, A BALANCED DAY IS BEST.

Prayer

Heavenly Father,
   Thank you for the gift of each new day. Help me to get the balance right between work, relaxation, play and sleep. I will then be able to give of my best to you, to my family and to my work. In Jesus's name, Amen.

Action this day

1 Review your usual pattern of activities.
2 Resolve to get a better balance between work, family, relaxation and sleep.

Thoughts for today

- Jesus said, 'Therefore do not worry about tomorrow, for tomorrow will worry about itself. Each day has enough trouble of its own.' (Matthew 6:34)
- Jesus said, 'Come with me by yourselves to a quiet place and get some rest.' (Mark 6:31)
- This is the day the Lord has made; let us rejoice and be glad in it.' (Psalm 118:24)

Lifestyle (2)
A balanced week, year, life

Yesterday we looked at the importance of a balanced lifestyle, and particularly at a balanced day, in protecting us from pressures.

Today we want to look beyond that.

A BALANCED WEEK IS IMPORTANT.

Experience has shown that a cycle of six days' activity and one of rest is most suitable for us, for our health, for our relationships and for productivity when we are working.

During the last world war, to try to increase production for the war machine, the ratio of rest days was reduced from 1-in-7 to 1-in-10. However, the health of workers deteriorated and production in fact decreased, and the 1-in-7 was reintroduced. Communist regimes have tried similar experiments with the same results.

When God created the world we learn that He 'worked' for six days and rested on the seventh. Some people believe that the days referred to are much longer periods – not, we think, borne out by the wording or the context. In any case, acknowledging the awesome power and wisdom of God, the question is not 'How could He manage it in just six days?', but rather 'Why did it take Him so long?' He could have done it in one day – or even instantaneously, if He had wished. The reason He took six days and then rested – was to set a pattern for us. Later He advises, through Moses, that WE should work for six days and rest on the seventh. This is the way He has made us to function, and we ignore this at our peril.

The temptations not to observe this God-given pattern are many and varied. Sometimes they are self-imposed – extra, overtime money needed to keep up with others; sometimes from the huge demands on us, even threats of redundancy, early retirement, demotion, cuts in pay let alone no promotion. So taking work home at the weekend becomes the norm rather than the exception. The working week becomes virtually seven days.

Sometimes we are too busy during the week for home maintenance, so that Sunday becomes a day of work – DIY, gardening, car washing and maintenance. Of course there are legitimate reasons for working on Sunday – the clergy and church leaders have to, hospital workers and others in public and safety services may need to. But it is imperative, if you are one of these, that you do rest for another day in the week.

NO ONE IS EXCLUDED FROM THE ONE-IN-SEVEN REST DAY CYCLE.

Taking the week as a whole including the weekend, it is good to have a balance in how we spend our time. As well as work, there should be time for rest, relaxation, and other interests or hobbies.

Some people, particularly some Christians, feel guilty if they are not busy working at something all the time, or if they are not engaged in some charity or Christian service during spare minutes. It is sensible and wise to

TAKE SOME TIME OFF DURING THE WEEK.

It is not being lazy or slothful.

If you spend much of your time in physical work, then balance this with relaxation periods of reading or on a holiday exercising your mind and resting your body. If, on the other hand, your main occupation is using brain rather than brawn, then, as long as you are otherwise healthy, balance this with exercise, like walking or a sport or gardening.

There should also be time for relaxation, listening to music, painting, watching TV or whatever turns you on. Gardening is excellent and has benefits other than just the exercise. According to the publication *Kew* in the summer of 1992, it helps people with emotional problems to realize that there are some things that are always outside human control! Indeed a new qualification in gardening therapy has been launched at the University of

Warwick, in conjunction with a charity, 'Horticultural Therapy'.

Don't forget time for your spouse, your children and your family, either.

BALANCED IS BEST.

If your circumstances allow, then owning a pet can be of great benefit to you. A report in the *Medical Journal of Australia* in 1992 showed that in people attending a health clinic, those who owned pets had lower blood pressure and lower blood fats; and according to an article in the *Journal of the Royal Society of Medicine* in 1991, acquiring a pet, either a dog or a cat, improved health significantly.

Perhaps it is difficult for you to achieve the kind of balanced lifestyle we have been advocating. You may be a busy mother, with little respite from demanding children and their needs. But balance for you is also important; time alone with husband or friends; time for a hobby or interest which stimulates your mind; time just to put your feet up.

If you have no nearby relatives and cannot afford a regular babysitter, might it be possible to find other parents in the same situation and come to an arrangement with them on a mutual help basis, so that you can have time off?

Perhaps you cannot get out much, or to work, so that a balance is difficult. But there are often voluntary services or groups or churches who will visit or take you for outings, and so some balance may be possible.

In the longer term, balance is also needed.

HOLIDAYS ARE IMPORTANT.

In some circles, taking a holiday from work is frowned on. 'The Chairman never takes a holiday, so why should you?' This is short-sighted and unwise, both for the health of the individual and his or her ability to combat pressures, but also for the longer-term health and productivity of the company. Nowadays too, with so much pressure, some people are afraid to go on holiday because of the backlog they will face on return. This is understandable but a break is necessary and will allow a refreshed body and mind to tackle the work with renewed zest.

The change is good especially if the holiday can provide a balance from your normal existence or main occupation. The holiday itself should be balanced and take in all the factors we have been discussing.

A holiday should be long enough to allow time for you to wind down. If you have been very busy and stressed, this may take about a week. During that period it is quite common for there to be a reaction. Your body has grown used to the 'stress' chemicals, and suddenly they have gone. This can lead to a degree of irritability itself – a kind of withdrawal effect. It is wise to realize this and be on your guard for it happening. The second week is really when the body and mind can benefit from the holiday. So two weeks is better than one. Better still is to have a third week, when your mind and body can begin to gear themselves up for a return to work and pressure.

If in addition you can build in a number of shorter breaks during the year, then this will all help to keep you fit and able to cope with pressures when they come.

Holidays don't need to be expensive. If you can afford time completely off, having everything done for you – great. If this is not possible, you may be able to arrange an exchange with someone in another church in another part of the country.

HOLIDAYS ARE PART OF GOD'S PLAN.

He built quite a number into His people's year when He gave them guidelines for living.

So far we have advocated a

BALANCED LIFESTYLE

as far as body and soul are concerned. But we are also made up of SPIRIT and this must be allowed for too.

A **daily** quiet time with God, for worship, prayer and reading His word will feed our spirit and allow it to grow.

A **weekly** time of worship, prayer and teaching with our fellow Christians, with times to remember the Lord's death and resurrection at communion, will keep our weeks in balance.

Giving time and attention for the spiritual parts of Christmas, Easter, Harvest and other special occasions will keep our year in balance too.

So a balanced lifestyle is important. Balanced days, weeks and years – balanced as far as body, soul and spirit are concerned.

Prayer

Dear Father,
You want me to lead a balanced life and I want to do your will.
Please help me to get my days, and my weeks and my years in balance.
Please help me to get my whole life in balance – body, soul and spirit. For Jesus's sake, Amen.

Action this day

1 Look at your average week. How balanced is it?
2 Plan next week so that it will be as balanced as possible.
3 Start arranging for Sundays, or another day in the week, to be a day of rest.
4 Plan short breaks into your year.
5 Plan a longer holiday next year.

Thoughts for today

- . . . so on the seventh day God rested from all His work. (Genesis 2:2)
- Six days you shall labour and do all your work, but the seventh day is a Sabbath to the Lord your God. On it you shall not do any work. (Exodus 20:9, 10)
- Then He said to them, 'The Sabbath was made for man, not man for the Sabbath.' (Mark 2:27)

The essentials of time management

The most important thing you will ever have to manage is time

Are your always rushed, never enough time for all you want to do, always trying to meet deadlines? You may be on the way to developing 'hurry sickness' and stress.

We have been looking at a healthy lifestyle as far as each day, each week and longer periods are concerned.

Now we move on to actual use of time.

Some people have more money and possessions than others, some more beauty, brains or brawn. But TIME is a commodity which we cannot buy, borrow or steal, which we cannot bank, save or hoard. We are all given it in exactly the same amount – the same minutes in an hour, hours in a day, days in a week – but we can decide how we spend it.

Do you spend time wisely? How much of it are you wasting? If you want to find out where the time goes, keep a record for a few days. Divide each day into twenty-four hours and then fill in the hours as accurately as you can.

Much has been written on time management. Good courses lasting from one day to one week are available. But there are only a few imporant principles to put into practice, and we have distilled these for you from much that has been written and said on this subject. More accurately, they involve 'self' management rather than 'time' management.

In planning your time:

1 Subtract the time you *must* spend daily on essential functions.

You will find that there are in fact few – like sleeping, eating, washing, bathing, working.

2 Decide on the big priorities in your life (we have already discussed some of these in Day 7), and *allocate* time for them. If prayer is of great importance then it is not enough to pray as you walk to the shops or drive to work. Yes, we must pray without ceasing and so you can pray at these times. But you should put aside time for this and the other important things in your life, such as time with God, your spouse, your children, rest and relaxation.

3 Plan your day. Someone has said 'Preparation prevents pressure. Procrastination produces it.' To help in your planning, pray about your daily priorities.

4 To have time for priorities, you may need to discard or certainly reduce the time spent on items of low importance. Most people spend 80 per cent of their time on the 20 per cent least important things.

   Do you spend two and a half hours a day watching TV? This is probably a low estimate – think about it. Keep an honest record for one week. You may be surprised. Two and a half hours a day equals seventeen and and a half hours a week, which equals over nine hundred hours a year. This is equivalent to almost twenty-six working weeks (assuming a working week of thirty-five hours). So this is the time you are spending in front of your set. We are not saying you should never sit down and relax and watch TV, but rather that you do keep a check on this insidious time consumer. It will help if you plan your viewing – as we hope you are getting into the habit of planning other activities and priorities.

5 There are only two other ways of making time for priorities – delegate when you can and look for ways of doing what you have to do more efficiently. Doing things more efficiently may mean giving up some time to plan and organize just how you do things. Not having a good filing system or not having things in their place can lose you much time if you have constantly to look for things you have misplaced.

   A FILING SYSTEM is better than A PILING SYSTEM but

you may feel you cannot give up time to get organized.

HOW ABOUT MAKING TIME BY MISSING YOUR LEAST FAVOURITE TV PROGRAMME FOR THE NEXT TWO WEEKS?

6 Concentrate on and do one thing at a time. Try to exclude from your mind the other things waiting to be done, until their time comes. Thinking about other things can distract you from the task being dealt with. This can lead to mistakes – in the end costing more time and effort to put right. It can lead to inefficiency because the task in hand takes longer to accomplish. Light concentrated through a glass burns, but light does not burn if it is dissipated.

We can learn from Jesus and His use of time. Despite the tremendous demands on Him, and the very limited time (three years) He had for His 'ministry', Jesus never appeared rushed or anxious or stressed. He knew what His primary task was and was not diverted from that. He only did what His heavenly Father wanted Him to do. He spent time alone with God. Despite the pressures to teach, preach and heal, He took time to rest, and relax, alone and with His friends. He spent time in exercise as He walked from place to place. He delegated.

Prayer

Lord,

Thank you for the gift of time. I admit that I have not been making best use of it. Please forgive me. I want you to be LORD of my time and my priorities. Please show me what I should cut down, and guide me as I plan my days as I want to do your will. In Jesus's name, Amen.

Action this day

1 Plan this week's TV viewing and stick to it.
2 Plan your time for today:
  – Discard very low priority items.
  – Make time for the big priorities.
3 Decide on one thing that you could do more efficiently. Think how you could do it better – plan in time to do what you need to organize it better.

Thoughts for today

- Jesus declared, '. . . I have come down from heaven not to do my will but to do the will of Him who sent me.' (John 6:38)
- Jesus said, 'Come with me by yourselves to a quiet place and get some rest.' (Mark 6:31)
- See also Exodus 18:13–27 – for the wonderful advice Moses's father-in-law, Jethro, gave him about delegation.

Who am I?

What we think of ourselves and what we are – our self-image – plays a very important part in our ability to cope with life's pressures and events, good or bad. A poor self-image will make us very vulnerable to pressures.

In counselling, we frequently encounter people who do not seem to know who they really are. They are out of touch with themselves and often have a hidden fear that any deep examination of their lives will result in them finding that 'the lights are on but no one is at home'; that there really is no one there, only a mask or shell covering up emptiness inside.

Others have an apparently good self-image, appearing confident and in charge of their lives. But often this is a front, covering up a deep insecurity and sense of inadequacy. Behind the façade they are just like the rest of us.

Indeed, we all have a poor self-image to some extent, and this can make us vulnerable to pressures. So it is important to know what makes up our self-image, how we develop it, and then see whether there is any hope for lasting change to it for the better.

Today we will spend some time looking at a simple model of how we develop a sense of 'self' and what self-image is composed of.

I am who I belong to

In life, the first and earliest sense of self depends on a growing awareness of being accepted and *belonging* to someone significant. Babies are born with this desire to belong, and during their first year this is the main area of identity being established. This sense of belonging, of being unconditionally accepted, wanted, loved, is conveyed initially by touch (the skin is the largest and most well developed sense organ in a baby), then by listening and then by sight. This need in a baby is so crucial to its survival that absence of contact or touch (through cuddling, etc.) can result in its death even though physically well nourished.

The mother or full-time carer is primarily responsible for establishing a strong sense of belonging in a baby.

I am what is valued in me

A sense of *self-worth* is the next area of self-image to be formed. This starts to emerge at two–three years of age, and both parents contribute to it. The toddler is picking up and internalizing parental approval of him directly and indirectly via parental values and standards. The degree to which parents appear to value and approve of the child's actions, thoughts and opinions that are expressions of its unique personality is the extent to which the child will feel worthwhile as an individual person.

I am what I can do

Children need to develop a sense of *competence* and ability to carry out what is expected of them, and to explore their talents and abilities to see whether they can make an impact on their world.

This begins roughly around the ages of six–seven. Often the father plays a significant role in affirming his children's competence and encouraging further developments of their abilities.

The next crucial stage in a person's development of identity comes during adolescence. Adolescents start to develop a sense of separateness from parents, and to rely on other things to develop further their sense of identity. However, these will all be laid down on the bedrock of self-image formed during childhood, usually during the first seven years of life.

The extent to which this foundation was well laid will largely determine how well the young teenager will form this separate identity, and how smoothly the transition to adulthood will be made.

Teenagers tend to derive a sense of **belonging** from within their peer groups, with a strong emphasis on appearance and dress to reinforce this sense of acceptance. It is very important to young people that they wear the 'right' clothes as far as their friends are concerned. The more insecure a youngster feels, the more he will be drawn to groups with a strong identity – this can be good or bad, either uniformed groups such as Scouts, Guides, etc., or non-uniformed, such as biker gangs and other teenage groups. Groups and gangs ease the teenager through the transition from parental dependency to independence.

Self-worth again is sought from peer approval, usually through status within the group: the higher the status, the greater the sense of worth. Positions of leadership and power amongst boys, and physical attractiveness amongst girls are common sources of worth.

Competence is measured through performance – often sporting or academic achievement in our culture. Other areas of competence such as character qualities of loyalty, helpfulness, consideration and perseverance are rarely valued or used as criteria of competence during the teens.

These same values are usually taken forward into adulthood, although probably altered to suit changing situations of full-time employment, marriage and parenthood. **Belonging** is usually primarily sought from marriage/romantic relationships, friendships and clubs or church life. **Worth** is acquired from career/work status, marital status, possessions, titles and professional status. **Competence** comes from achievements, awards, promotion, sporting achievements, work and how good we are as parents.

Inadequate fulfilment of these areas of self-image can result in painful feelings of being unacceptable, unlovable, worthless, inadequate and a failure as a human being.

Feelings of hostility, anger and resentment, which can be expressed outwards in violence, aggression and rages, or inwards as depression, can result from feeling we do not belong.

Guilt is usually associated with worthlessness, feelings of being a mistake, needing to apologize for living, and feeling responsible for everything that goes wrong in life.

Deep-rooted anxiety and fear of failure flow from feelings of inadequacy.

A poor self-image results in a belief that we cannot cope with life, leading to increased attempts to try harder, with rising inner tension and conflict. Sustained failure to feel good about ourselves can end up in disillusionment and frustration, together with effects of stress. These feelings are often deeply buried and out of the range of our conscious awareness, usually only surfacing when a pressure or situation exposes them through our reaction to it.

However, in addition to all the above, it is important to point out that the formation of our self-image is not entirely dependent on the people and events of our developing years. We too have to take some responsibility for the way we think of ourselves.

The crucial thing about our self-image is that:

It is not based on what I think I am;
It is not based on what **YOU** think I am;
It IS BASED ON WHAT **I THINK YOU THINK I AM!**

It is rather like looking at ourselves in a distorted funfair mirror, wearing a pair of thick-lensed glasses. So whatever our self-image is, it is unlikely to be correct because it is dependent upon two distorted and fallible reflections of ourselves.

But what we really need is a true, undistorted objective view of ourselves. If we want this true reflection of ourselves, we need to ask someone we can absolutely trust, who knows the real truth about who and what we are, without bias, and yet who is not going to destroy us with that information. Not only that, but that someone must be a person whose opinion is more important to us than anyone else's, so that we will be open and willing to believe what they say about us, no matter how we might feel about ourselves.

DO YOU KNOW ANYONE LIKE THAT?

Tomorrow, we will explore ways in which we can change our self-image for the better, and bring hope to those who struggle under the burden of a poor, damaged or inadequate self-image.

Prayer

Heavenly Father,
Please help me to be honest about how I see myself, so that I can move on to know the truth about me. Although it is frightening to do so, I trust you to be with me as I carry out this examination of myself, believing it is in your will to do so. Please may your Holy Spirit help me gain insight into how this affects my relationship with you and with others. In Jesus's name, Amen.

Action this day

1 Think about what you really believe about yourself: acceptable or unacceptable, lovable or unlovable, 'good' or 'bad', worthless or worthwhile, capable and competent or inadequate and a failure. Grade each category on a scale of 1–10, with 1 being totally unacceptable and 10 totally acceptable.
2 Think about how you might have developed this idea of yourself – what were the 'mirrors' in your life and what did you think they were saying about you?
3 Think about how this self-image is affecting the way you cope with pressures in your life and with your relationships with others.

Thoughts for today

- Let us examine our ways and test them. (Lamentations 3:40)
- Examine yourselves to see whether you are in the faith; test yourselves. (2 Corinthians 13:5)
- And this is my prayer: that your love may abound more and more in knowledge and depth of insight, so that you may be able to discern what is best and may be pure and blameless until the day of Christ. (Philippians 1:9, 10)
- And if you call out for insight and cry aloud for understanding . . . Then you will understand what is right and just and fair – every good path. For wisdom will enter your heart and knowledge will be pleasant to your soul. Discretion will protect you, and understanding will guard you. (Proverbs 2:3, 9–11)
- Reflect on what I am saying, for the Lord will give you insight into all this. (2 Timothy 2:7)

Day 12

How to change your self-image

Yesterday we saw that a poor self-image can make us vulnerable to pressures. We saw too that our self-image is based on what we think others think we are, and that many of us have a poor self-image. We suggested that in order to start to change our self-image to a true one we need to find a trustworthy, faithful, loving and all-knowing friend who can accurately reflect back to us the truth about ourselves. Not only that, but we must also then choose to believe that person's evaluation as being accurate and true, and accept it for ourselves.

Unfortunately, there is no one on earth who can be trusted as far as that, as all people are fallible and have limited knowledge. However, we do know a man who can! That is Jesus Christ, our maker and God. You see, our Maker's Manual is the place to find the true mirror of who we are. We need to find out what God thinks of us and to accept that as the truth.

The Bible tells us that God made man, Adam, in His own image and that it was GOOD. However, when Adam chose to go his own way and reject God, the perfect image was smashed and broken. All Adam's offspring inherit his broken image from conception. This means that we do not function properly, in the way we were designed to. With a broken image, man no longer *belongs* to God in an intimate relationship, has no value or *worth* that he can offer to God for His approval, and he is totally *incapable* of pleasing God through anything he does or achieves. An identity transplant is required, nothing less.

But, the good news is that

GOD WANTS TO GIVE US A BRAND NEW IDENTITY
AND SELF-IMAGE.

Through faith in Jesus's death and resurrection on our behalf,
our old identity from Adam is destroyed and we are born again
with a new identity, which is perfect, holy and righteous.

As a result of receiving this new identity,

WE NOW **BELONG** TO GOD AS OUR FATHER

in an intimate, warm and loving relationship, totally secure in
this relationship for eternity, a member of his royal family, son
and heir of God and co-heir with Jesus. We are now no longer
'sinners' who sin, but 'saints' who also can still sin but no longer
have to. Now our *appearance* to God is not the dirty, filthy
sinner, who is unacceptable to Him in His purity and holiness,
but rather as the washed, pure, radiant and holy child. Jesus
reminded Peter at the last supper, when He washed his feet, that
Peter had been washed by his faith in Christ, and that he
therefore needed only his feet washed (which symbolized the
baptism into the Church family). So it is with all Christians.

We can now approach the heavenly throne and be found
acceptable to God because of what Jesus has done for us and in
us. Paul reminds the Corinthian church that although many of
them came from immoral and wicked backgrounds, and as such
were totally unacceptable to God, 'But you were washed, you
were sanctified, you were justified in the name of the Lord Jesus
Christ and by the Spirit of God' (1 Corinthians 6:11). 'It does
not, therefore, depend on man's desire or effort, but on God's
mercy' (Romans 9:16). The love of our Father drives out
hostility and bitterness related to our lack of belonging and
insecurity (Romans 8:39).

The value of any object is directly related to how much anyone
is prepared to pay to obtain it. So

OUR **WORTH** IS NOW MEASURED BY THE PRICE
GOD WAS WILLING TO PAY TO OBTAIN US – THE
LIFE OF HIS ONLY SON.

God considers us to be so precious that He was willing to die in order to obtain us for His own. This is not a performance-based worth! This is an unconditional, unreserved and unearned worth. God approves of us because we put our faith in His Son and on that basis alone. Just as we depend upon our status to gain approval from others, now our status is as saints and royal sons of God. We are co-heirs with Christ, approved and valued by the King of kings and Lord of lords. What higher status can we acquire? However, because this is given entirely as a gift from God, no one can boast and no one has an advantage over anyone else as far as God is concerned.

God not only valued us enough to die for us, but also enough to go through the agonies of bearing all the sin of the world, enduring our severe punishment and plunging into the depths of hell to rescue us and make us His own. How would you have felt as a child if you knew your parents valued you to this extent?

We can stop anxiously and guiltily striving to win God's approval. WE HAVE IT ALREADY!

Our new spirit is now righteous in God's sight, and our guilt at never matching up to impossible standards can now be replaced by FORGIVENESS FOR THE PAST, PRESENT AND FUTURE failures and sins.

However, have we got what it takes to please God and to fulfil His expectations of us? Well, no, not in our own strength we haven't, as any of you struggling to be good Christians can testify. Jesus also reminds us that without Him we can do nothing. But,

GOD GIVES US HIS HOLY SPIRIT WHO MAKES US **COMPETENT** TO FULFIL HIS EXPECTATIONS AND COMMANDMENTS.

'For it is God who works in you to will and to act according to His good purpose.' (Philippians 2:13)

We no longer have to strive in our own strength to meet God's expectations of us. We can rest in the knowledge that whatever God calls us to do, He equips us for it, both through natural talents and abilities working under and in the power of the Holy

Spirit. So **fear of failure** can be replaced by a quiet confidence and sureness that we can succeed in doing God's will for us. 'Not that we are competent in ourselves to claim anything for ourselves, but our competence comes from God. He has made us competent as ministers of a new covenant.' (2 Corinthians 3:5,6)

So, if this is what the Bible tells us about ourselves, what are **you** going to do about it? Are you going to continue to believe and hold onto your old self-image, with all its problems, or are you going to risk losing it and trusting what the word of God says, and choose to believe and base your life and actions on this wonderful truth?

THE CHOICE IS YOURS.

What need is there for a poor self-image when you have been given such a wonderful new identity in and through Jesus Christ?

Prayer

Heavenly Father,
I praise you for what you have done in order to give me this wonderful new identity. I confess that I have not completely realized what this means to me, and I have been living with the old self-image for a long time. Help me now to let go of it as far as possible, to shed the 'old me' and to believe and accept by faith the 'new me' that you say I am. Then show me, one step at a time, how this will change what I do and say to others, and how I deal with pressures when they come. For Jesus's sake, Amen.

Action this day

1 Read and meditate on the Bible passages below.
2 Personalize them, using your own name.

3 Remind yourself DAILY
   a) that you are LOVED BY, BELONG TO AND ARE ACCEPTABLE TO GOD
   b) that you are PRECIOUS, VALUED AND WORTH-WHILE TO GOD
   c) that you CAN DO EVERYTHING THAT GOD WANTS YOU TO DO THROUGH THE POWER OF HIS HOLY SPIRIT.

   This is the same as putting on the armour of God. (Ephesians 6:13–18)
4 Ask God to open your eyes to see other people in the same way as He sees you and them. (Love others as you have been loved by God.)

Thoughts for today

- How great is the love the Father has lavished on us, that we should be called children of God! And that is what we are! (1 John 3:1)
- For you know that it was not with perishable things such as silver or gold that you were redeemed from the empty way of life handed down to you from your forefathers, but with the precious blood of Christ, a lamb without blemish or defect. (1 Peter 1:18–19)
- For you have been born again, not of perishable seed, but of imperishable, through the living and enduring word of God. (1 Peter 1:23)
- I am the vine; you are the branches. If a man remains in me and I in him, he will bear much fruit; APART FROM ME YOU CAN DO NOTHING. (John 15:5)
- I have learned the secret of being content in any and every situation, whether well fed or hungry, whether living in plenty or in want. I can do everything through him who gives me strength. (Philippians 4:12, 13)

Deep personal needs

An area closely related to self-image is that of our deep personal needs.

God created us to depend upon a source outside ourselves to sustain us. God is the only self-existent being. We, as dependent beings, have been created with needs in our lives, needs that must be fulfilled for us to be able to function at our best and to cope with the pressures of life.

We have three levels of need in our lives:

CASUAL NEEDS, which we can live without relatively easily; these relate to our comfort and convenience.

CRITICAL NEEDS, such as food and drink, clothing and shelter, and also significant relationships, without which it will become difficult and painful to function.

CRUCIAL NEEDS, which absolutely require satisfaction if we are to continue to function as persons. If these needs are not met, it will spell deep personal pain and breakdown for us, and eventually we shall die as persons.

The Bible often refers to these personal needs in us as 'thirsts', 'hungers' or 'longings', and nowhere does it condemn us or put us down for having them. They are part of our make-up – rather like a petrol tank in a car. The problems arise in our lives not because we have these needs, but rather if they are not met.

So what are these crucial needs in our lives, these deep thirsts and longings? We have basically three main needs:

SECURITY – the need to be totally and unconditionally loved without needing to change in order to obtain such love, a love that can neither be earned nor lost. Women seem to depend on this for fulfilment more than men do.

SELF-WORTH – the need to feel that our lives have value; that we are desired by a significant other person who values us unconditionally for ourselves, without our having to perform in order to achieve it.

SIGNIFICANCE – the need to feel that our lives have meaning and purpose, that we are moving purposefully towards a significant goal and that we are adequate to accomplish that purpose. There is the desire to have an impact on another person and our world, which will last through eternity. Men seem to depend on this for their fulfilment more than women do.

Filling these needs is what motivates our behaviour and influences our choices, and is the driving force of our lives. When situations occur that threaten or undermine the fulfilment of these needs, we suffer from the effects of stress, or strain.

Where do we normally look to have these needs filled?

Security and love are often sought from parents, marital relationships, significant friendships, romantic relationships and from our children.

Self-worth is sought from other people's approval. The closer the person is to us, the more self-worth we demand from them through their approval of us. Ways of getting approval from others come through our position in society, status, performance, doing what other people want, by behaving in a certain way, money, possessions, clothes, religious performance and outward show of respectability or piety, good works, and being needed by others.

Significance is sought from work, career, professional associations, power, possessions, clubs and affiliations, positions of leadership, attendance at church, functions and positions within the church, our 'ministry', use of spiritual gifts and being seen as a 'spiritual' person.

We often fear and resist change as it may undermine or threaten these sources of filling our personal needs (unless, of course, the change promises to increase those things we depend upon). Anger, pain, anxiety, fear and guilt are often emotions that arise when these sources are threatened. We increase our attempts to avoid this pain by trying to keep things as they are or by changing them back to what we want with increasing effort and stress – the self-protection reaction.

If we are unable to alter circumstances to suit us, then we may adopt all kinds of inner self-protective defensive reactions to shield us from experiencing the pain of unmet needs. These can take a myriad of forms, like eating disorders, neuroses, phobias, anxiety attacks, and physical symptoms (the psyche will often 'dump' unresolved emotions and pain into the body when it is overloaded), depression, behavioural problems, violence, aggression, physical and emotional breakdown.

Our spiritual lives suffer increasingly as we continue to struggle to control our lives, and we will find prayer and communion with God almost impossible at these times.

Ever since Adam and Eve decided to meet their deepest personal needs apart from God, mankind has had a great aversion to experiencing its deep dependency on God, and considers it to be a sign of contemptible weakness and inadequacy, to be avoided at all costs. A successful person in the world's view is one who appears not to have any of these needs at all, and is able to operate confidently and independently, without apparent need for anyone or anything else. The rest of us just feel pathetic and failures when we become aware of our needs, and cannot face up to them without experiencing either deep shame or profound self-contempt.

When one source of meeting our needs is denied us, we will switch over to another, and another and another, in a desperate attempt to avoid facing our dependency, until they run out.

The big problem with these sources for meeting our deep needs is that they are not reliable or dependable, and sometimes are downright harmful. So we are basing our very lives on things that can and often will let us down; we may lose our spouse through divorce or death; our children may rebel and leave home or reject us; our jobs are increasingly insecure; we can lose our home through repossession, fire or weather damage. Other people's approval becomes increasingly difficult as we widen our circle of contacts and acquaintances, and we discover that we can never please or impress all of the people all of the time and so on.

In Jeremiah 2:13, God calls this inclination of ours to depend on created things to meet our deep needs 'digging broken cisterns', and condemns us for doing so. In the desert, wandering tribes dug holes in the ground to capture any rain, dew and condensation or water percolating through the limestone, rather like the dew ponds on the Sussex Downs. Though the water may be kept sweet for a time if it is looked after, it is often filthy and cannot be compared to the pure water from living fountains.

The cisterns are also easily broken and the water leaks away. So as far as God is concerned, to look to the created order to fulfil our deep thirsts is like stubbornly preferring to drink from a muddy puddle than from a clear mountain stream.

As you will realize, this dependency on things or people not within our control or who are not reliable makes us very vulnerable, and we can easily be destroyed when and if we lose any of them. Imagine if we had been in Job's place when he lost everything. Could we have coped with it like he did? Jesus urges us not to depend upon things that can rust, be destroyed by moths or be stolen or taken away from us. He considers this to be the attitude and behaviour of pagans, not of the people of God.

If you do not want to be vulnerable to loss or change, then please consider the things in your life that you depend upon for your sense of security, self-worth and significance. Test them to see whether they are reliable, eternal or of temporary existence.

Tomorrow, we will look at where we can find a truly reliable and dependable source for our deepest needs and how to make this source a reality in our lives.

Prayer

Heavenly Father,
Please help me to look with complete honesty at the things on which I am building my life. Please give me insight about how I react when these things are being challenged or are changing. I really want to be completely open with you so that you can have free reign in my life. For Jesus's sake, Amen.

Action this day

1 Complete the following sentences (you may have more than one answer to each question).

I (would) feel secure when ....

I (would) feel loved when/if ....

I (would) feel valued/worthwhile as a person when/if..............

I (would) feel significant/important/with meaning and purpose when/if..

2 How do you/would you feel if you lost any of the above or if they were threatened in any way?

3 How dependable or reliable are any of them? Do you have absolute control over any of them?

4 What would you do/do you do to protect them? Is that what Jesus would do in your position?

Thoughts for today

- Then Jesus said to His disciples: 'Therefore I tell you, do not worry about your life, what you will eat; or about your body, what you will wear. Life is more than food, and the body more than clothes . . . Who of you by worrying can add a single hour to his life? Since you cannot do this very little thing, why do you worry about the rest? . . . For the pagan world runs after all such things, and your Father knows that you need them [*critical needs*].' (Luke 12: 22, 23, 25, 26, 30)

- My people have committed two sins: They have forsaken me, the spring of living water, and have dug their own cisterns, broken cisterns that cannot hold water. (Jeremiah 2:13)

- Blessed are the meek [*those who are fully aware of their weakness and dependency*], for they shall inherit the earth. Blessed are those who *hunger* and *thirst* for righteousness for they will be filled. (Matthew 5:5, 6)

Day 14

How to satisfy your deep personal needs

Yesterday we saw that we all have deep needs which are crucial to our functioning as personal beings – security, self-worth, significance – and that we tend to meet these needs from various sources in the world, which in turn tend to be undependable, unreliable and beyond our control. We also saw that God warns us about this, and indeed takes a very dim view of the sources we use to meet these needs. In Jeremiah, He condemns this action as sin. This is irrespective of how respectable, natural and 'right' the source of meeting our needs might be. We often justify things in our life because they aren't 'wrong' or sinful things, such as depending on our spouse to make us feel loved and secure, or on our spiritual or Christian or charity work to make us feel worthwhile, or on our position or gifting in the church, to make us feel significant.

However, God says that depending on ANYTHING other than Him for meeting these needs is sinful, no matter what it is. In other words, this is not the way He made us to function, so it is not in our best interests nor in His will for us to do so. It is rather like buying a car designed to run on petrol, but into which we insist on putting diesel, alcohol, methylated spirits or any other kind of combustible fuel. The car may function well for a time. But eventually the engine will start to malfunction because it is not designed to operate with anything other than petrol. We would all agree that anyone who ignores the manufacturer's specification could be considered a 'fool' for stubbornly going his own way. Unfortunately, we are all at it in our own lives.

God usually only gets our attention when pressures come along and we become aware of how vulnerable we are when we suffer from effects of stress. God wants to use this very time to show us that our 'broken cistern' has run out and that we need to come to Him for filling and satisfaction. Sadly, rather than humbly acknowledging our weakness and inadequacy to our loving Father, we usually tend to rush off to dig another 'broken cistern' by finding something else that will either serve the same purpose or will keep us going, albeit inadequately.

Because God loves us so much, He is committed to getting our attention and changing the sources of meeting our deep needs from things of the world to Him alone. We are beings designed to be personally empowered and fed on God alone. He is the spring of living water, pure, untainted, unlimited and totally satisfying to our souls. He alone can feed and satisfy the hunger in our souls for security, worth and meaning, not through anything we do but rather through a direct personal relationship with Him. Christians often misinterpret the Bible when it says that God will meet all our needs, by believing that He will do it by supplying 'broken cisterns'. For example, we may say to ourselves: 'I need to feel loved, and having a husband will satisfy that need in me, so, Lord, please supply me with a husband, because you promise to meet all my needs.' You could well be disappointed in the outcome! GOD DOES NOT PROMISE TO MEET OUR NEEDS IN THIS WAY.

He promises to do it through our relationship with Jesus Christ and through living for Him alone. Through the work of the Holy Spirit in our lives, we can by faith experience the reality of profound filling of the longings of our hearts, miraculously, supernaturally.

WE CAN BE CONTENT IN ANY AND EVERY SITUATION.

Jesus promised the woman at the well in Samaria that He could fill the thirst of her soul for love and affirmation in a way that her five 'husbands' had been unable to do. The promise stands for all of us.

If we are fully depending upon Jesus to meet all our crucial needs, then if and when we lose any of the other important things in our lives, which should be now relegated to the realm of CRITICAL NEED, although it will hurt and grieve us, it will not destroy us and we can still function in a healthy, responsible way in response to such an event. Paul had learned this secret, as he stated in Philippians 4, that he could be content in ANY and EVERY situation, whether in want or abundance, poverty or riches.

Larry Crabb, a highly respected biblical counsellor, compares the difference between having Jesus as the source of our crucial needs, and having other things as sources, to being rather like the difference between a five-foot fall and a thousand-foot fall. If we are depending upon Christ for our security, self-worth and significance, then losing our job, spouse or children etc., cannot destroy us, even though it can deeply hurt us, rather like the injury from a five-foot fall. However, if our lives totally depend upon those relationships and things, if we do lose them, it can be devastating and potentially destroying – like falling one thousand feet.

Unfortunately, none of us like to admit, even to ourselves, that we even have these needs. We tend to be ashamed and contemptuous of those feelings in our lives and will do our very best to bury them. This is often why we will not turn to the Lord when things are going wrong in our lives, as we cannot bear to face up to our needs. We seem to know instinctively that turning to face God will result in our becoming painfully aware of how weak and vulnerable we are, and we are either too proud to accept this, or deeply afraid of incurring God's contempt for us if He gets to find out our weakness and inadequacy. This is especially the case if someone grew up in a family that was very contemptuous of any signs of weakness or need in others. That person will carry this view into his relationship with God, and humility and honesty will be seen as very threatening.

Yet Paul views his weakness, infirmity, humiliations, persecutions, hardships as things to BOAST about rather than be ashamed of. He continually exults in his weakness, because he knows that when he is weak then he is strong. In 2 Corinthians 11:21–29 Paul claims to possess all the things that the world views as making a man successful and significant, yet later in Philippians 3:7–9, he states that he considers these things to be 'rubbish', garbage, a loss to him, compared with his relationship with Christ. His greatness as a human being came solely from his relationship with Jesus, and from no other source.

THE ONLY WAY to experience and know God's power and presence and filling in our lives IS TO BE WILLING TO ADMIT TO OUR WEAKNESS, DEPENDENCY AND NEED.

Pride and fear are our two most implacable enemies, and they need to be ruthlessly dealt with if we wish to function in the way we were made to.

Pride is the foolish belief that we are capable of making our lives fulfilled by our own efforts and resources, and fear is the foolish belief that our lives will be destroyed or devastated if we fail to acquire those things that we believe make our lives worthwhile.

Only we ourselves can choose whether to walk past the 'muddy puddle' of the world's resources and depend upon the 'living spring' of God's fulfilment. No one else can make that choice for us. WE CAN CHOOSE NOT TO DEPEND UPON GOD, AND WE HAVE THE POWER TO CHOOSE TO BE TOTALLY DEPENDENT UPON GOD. And He holds US responsible for the choice we make.

See, I set before you today life and prosperity, death and destruction . . . This day I call heaven and earth as witnesses against you that I have set before you life and death, blessings and curses. Now CHOOSE LIFE, so that you and your children may LIVE, and that you may love the Lord your God, listen to His voice, and hold fast to HIM. For the Lord IS YOUR LIFE, and He will give you many years in the land He swore to give to your fathers, Abraham, Isaac and Jacob. (Deuteronomy 30:15, 19, 20)

Prayer

Heavenly Father,

I admit that I have been depending on many other things to make my life content and worthwhile. I see now that you did not make me to function in this way and that is why I suffer when these things are taken away or threatened. I want to be different from now on. Please show me the things I am depending on and help me to change to depending upon you alone for my deep needs.

Thank you, Father, that you do not despise me or have contempt for me because I am weak and needy, but that you are delighted when I come honestly and humbly to you to confess my needs and ask you to fill them for me. I CHOOSE LIFE FROM YOU ALONE FROM NOW ON. For Jesus's sake, Amen.

Action this day

1 Take from yesterday's actions the list of things that you have identified as making you feel secure, worthwhile and significant, confess them to the Lord, and repent of using them to meet these needs.

Ask the Lord Himself to come into those areas of your life and fill them with His presence and love, and BE ASSURED THAT HE WILL DO IT.

2 If you are stressed at the moment, ask yourself:
  a) what is the pressure causing the stress?
  b) what deep need – security, self-worth or significance – is being threatened or has been threatened by this pressure?

Then decide to have this need met directly from God – ask Him to meet it.

3 Every time you feel stressed, irritable and tense, ask yourself what deep need is being threatened or whether you are being self-protective against some pain or other threat. Identify your self-protective response and confess it to God. Trust

Him to protect you, whilst you commit yourself to act responsibly, patiently and lovingly in response to the pressure or stress.

Thoughts for today

- Jesus answered, 'Everyone who drinks this water will be thirsty again, but whoever drinks the water I give him will never thirst. Indeed, the water I give him will become in him a spring of water welling up to eternal life.' (John 4:13, 14)
- Blessed is he who has regard for the weak; the Lord delivers him in times of trouble. (Psalm 41:1)
- As the deer pants for streams of water, so my soul pants for you, O God. My soul thirsts for God, for the living God. (Psalm 42:1, 2)
- Do not work for food that spoils, but for food that endures to eternal life, which the Son of Man will give you. (John 6:27)
- Then Jesus declared, 'I am the bread of life. He who comes to me will never go hungry, and he who believes in me will never be thirsty.' (John 6:35)

What type of person are you?

Type A: the harm – the answer

Attempts have been made to 'type' people according to how they are, act and behave. In turn your type can have an important bearing on how you and your body react to pressures.

Typical Type 'A's live in the fast lane. He or she is always in a hurry, trying to do more than one thing at a time, impatient, very ambitious and often a workaholic; the kind of driver who sits right on your tail, flashing his lights and pulling out to try to overtake you at the least opportunity; and phones you from his car to say he will be a few minutes late as he is furious to be stuck in a traffic jam.

When you phone them you can hear them typing into their computer or word processor as they talk to you. They do not stop to eat, but either have a sandwich in the car or read or carry on business through each meal.

Even when they should be relaxing on the golf course they are talking business. They love pressure and stress, in fact seem to thrive on it. They seem addicted to adrenalin. Some Type 'A's can be quite hostile. They become easily irritated by other people's mistakes, even quite small ones. They are often very critical, finding it difficult to compliment other people, but are proud of their own standards and ideals; they are often contemptuous of others who are not as clever or good, or hardy as they themselves; they are often suspicious, and find it difficult to trust anyone. They don't laugh easily but are prone to expletives and using obscenities.

Although Type 'A's usually seem to be 'with it' people, appear confident, sometimes to the point of arrogance or hostility, deep down they are often insecure. They believe that their worth, and other people's worth, depends on achievements. Their fear of failure is often what motivates them and accounts for much of their behaviour. One of their other fears is that justice in the world may not prevail, and they are cynical about anyone having basic moral principles. They also fear that they will not get their share of whatever good is going, and that whatever it is will run out before their turn comes, and this can lead to impatience and hostility.

Type 'A's are very goal-orientated. Their satisfaction comes from a task well done, a mission completed, an objective reached, a problem solved. All these give them a real buzz. However, much of life is taken up with the doing rather than the completing – the journey rather than the arrival. It is wise therefore not to miss out on much of life by always having our eyes focused on the end, the achievement. There is satisfaction and pleasure from completing a project, but the actual completion is short-lived compared with the time involved all the way through. It is good to enjoy the moment when we have completed decorating a room and can stand back and admire our work. But it is even better if we can remember to enjoy the hours as we clean and paper and paint. It is good to enjoy the moment when we have completed mowing the lawn, but don't forget to look for and become aware of the basic pleasure to be found in actually mowing the grass.

Recent research has identified one of the qualities that make 'average' people excel. It is what Dr George Vaillant, a psychiatrist studying career paths, calls 'the capacity to postpone, but not forgo, gratification'. Unfortunately, many Type 'A's or 'fast trackers' expect too much too soon, and because they only get a buzz when the task is completed, when rewards don't materialize instantly they may become frustrated and unhappy and give up too soon, looking for other sources of reward and gratification.

Although there is not total agreement about the fate of Type 'A's, it does still seem, especially if they are also 'AHA' –

Angry, Hostile and Aggressive – that they are more likely to develop early high blood pressure and heart problems than are their more placid and slower counterpart Type 'B'.

Companies love Type 'A's because of their obsessive behaviour about work and perfection, but lose interest when they burn themselves out at an early age.

Life would be dull if we were all the same, and God has created us as unique individuals. We need Type 'A's *and* Type 'B's. Most people are a combination of the two – fairly balanced – and this is good.

However, if you are Type 'A', especially AHA, and want to avoid health complications, then you need to change your behaviour and slow down.

1 Make sure you take time to do the relaxation exercises regularly. As well as calming you down, they will begin slowly to change your outlook and behaviour.
2 Do one thing at a time.
3 Cut back on your schedule if it is overloaded.
4 Accept what you cannot change.
5 Accept delays – try even to enjoy them. In most cases you cannot affect the cause and you certainly can't by fretting.
6 Leave more time to do things, leave for church, the station, the plane earlier than you usually do.
7 Smile more. Talk less. Listen more.
8 Enjoy the journey as well as the arriving.

If you do not begin to do these things now, then you may HAVE TO after your first or next heart attack.

Unfortunately, if you are a typical Type 'A', you find it very hard to change your behaviour, and what is needed is a change from the inside – a real change in attitude and outlook.

This is possible, especially if you are still functioning according to days −3, −2, −1.

Prayer

Heavenly Father,
Thank you for the gifts and talents you have given me, and for the desire and ability to get things done. Please forgive me always being in a hurry and for my impatience and intolerance. Open my eyes to see that the meek shall inherit the earth, not Type 'A's. Show me that I can trust you to supply my daily needs and that I need not strain to achieve as my future is in your hands. Please quieten my spirit and mind and body. I now place this day and every day in your hands, for you to live in and through me in wonderful serenity. For Jesus sake, Amen.

Action this day

1 Resolve to enjoy your first delay today.
2 Stop in the middle of each thing you do today, and decide that you are going to enjoy it.
3 Compliment someone – sincerely!
4 Smile, NOW!
5 Begin to make these and the other hints for Type 'A's habits in your life.

Thoughts for today

- Be still, and know that I am God. (Psalm 46:10)
- And my God will supply all your needs according to His glorious riches in Christ Jesus. (Philippians 4:19)
- My times are in your hands. (Psalm 31:15)
- 'For I know the plans I have for you', declares the Lord, 'plans to prosper you and not to harm you, plans to give you hope and a future.' (Jeremiah 29:11)
- Blessed are the meek, for they will inherit the earth. (Matthew 5:5)

A special prayer for Type 'A's:

LORD, grant me the strength to change that which needs changing; the courage to accept that which cannot be changed, and the wisdom to know the difference. Amen.

Bitterness and resentment

The harm – the answer

Bitterness and resentment smouldering away can affect our body chemicals, our peace of mind and the health of our bodies.

Some people have become bitter and resentful because of things that have happened to them. They've been let down, rejected, disappointed, ignored, passed over, neglected, abused. The insults may have been real or imagined, or just exaggerated. Grudges have been born, fuelled and nurtured.

Others seem to have a generally bitter nature or attitude, believing that life owes them a living.

People who are bitter or resentful or who bear grudges are:

NEVER, EVER PEOPLE.

I will never ever forget.
I will never ever forgive.
I will never ever change.
Never, ever again, will I speak to . . .
Never, ever again, will I say I'm sorry.
Never, ever again, will I trust . . .
I will never, ever trust anyone again.

They are also:

'WHY'S' PEOPLE – NOT 'WISE' PEOPLE.

Why me?
Why didn't they?
Why did they?

Why has my husband/wife left me?
Why have I been passed over for promotion?
Why are some people more successful than I am?
Why have I never found a partner?
Why have I never had children?
Why does God never answer/listen to me?

There is often envy or jealousy of others. Trust in people completely disappears. Bitterness can give way to cynicism. Speech and looks take on a perpetual sneer. There is no joy, no deep peace. People like this become obsessed by their feelings.

Those feelings can turn outwards to family or church, or become vendettas towards former friends, giving rise to thoughts of revenge. The feelings can be infectious and can spread throughout an organization, office, community or church.

Or the feelings can turn inwards and become like a canker or running sore. Chronic damage to mind and body can ensue.

These emotions are self-destructive. People are consumed by such feelings. Job says 'Resentment kills a fool.' (Job 5:2)

There is an antidote but it is not easy to take. Not everyone is prepared to follow the instructions for cure. They are

CONFESS, REPENT, FORGIVE AND RECONCILE.

If we have been bearing grudges and resentments we have been harming ourselves and it is WRONG, no matter what the provocation or the circumstances. The Lord, whom we follow and want to become like, when they had rejected Him, taunted Him, ridiculed Him, mocked Him, spat at Him, flayed Him and crucified Him – *all unjustly* – said, 'Father, forgive them.' (Luke 23:34) We are expressly told that we must forgive. 'Forgive as the Lord forgave you.' (Colossians 3:13) 'Forgive, and you will be forgiven.' (Luke 6:37) There is no 'Forgive if you can'. In the parable of the unforgiving servant, the king threw the unmerciful servant into gaol until he should pay back all he owed, and Jesus warned, 'This is how my heavenly Father will treat each of you unless you forgive your brother from your heart.' (Matthew 18:21–35)

Again, in the Lord's Prayer we are told to ask forgiveness from

God to the extent that we are willing to forgive others who have sinned against us. The implication is that we will not be forgiven if we will not forgive others, and that leads to grave consequences for us.

FORGIVENESS IS NOT AN OPTION FOR CHRISTIANS.

If you are bearing a grudge, or feel bitter or resentful

CONFESS IT TO GOD, REPENT AND FORGIVE

asking for God's forgiveness for you.

Some people say, 'I do not feel forgiving'. This is not the point. We are not commanded to *feel forgiving* but to *forgive*. True, we cannot generate feelings of forgiveness, but it is to be an act of the will, at this stage.

Some say, 'I cannot forgive'. What they really mean is 'I won't'. We are all in charge of our behaviour. We can decide to put out a hand, to open our mouths and say, 'I forgive you'. Our forgiveness may not be accepted. This also is not the point. We are following instructions, discharging our duty. If the other party does not accept then this is his or her ongoing problem.

Some make the excuse 'I do not feel forgiving and so I do not want to be hypocritical by saying "I forgive".' Well, yes, you will be hypocritical to your feelings, but if you are acting in obedience to God's will, what is wrong with that? Scripture does not command us to change our feelings before we act, but rather to be obedient to God as an act of the will.

If we take whatever action seems appropriate – a handshake, a hug, a word, a letter – God will honour our obedience. He will forgive us, and healing changes will begin to take place in our mind and body. If we want to forgive, we can ask God and leave it to Him, in time, to replace the bitter feelings with those of love and care. Forgiveness, especially for very great wrongs and hurts, can be a process before the feelings change, but constant self-reminding of our choice to forgive is necessary each time hurt and pain surface.

SEE IF IT WORKS!

You will feel released. Joy and peace will surely come.

Whether our overtures of forgiveness are accepted or not, it is important, when appropriate, to go on to make whatever restitution is needed, or to take whatever action is needed at that time to make reconciliation possible, to open lines of communication: 'Whenever you want to come back, the door is open.' 'When you want to speak, I am at the end of the phone.' 'I will not obstruct things any more.' God will honour your attitude and your actions.

Warning

Do not speak in forgiveness to anyone who either does not know that you are harbouring a grudge or criticism against him or her or who is oblivious to the fact that you feel they have wronged you. This is unwise, unkind and unnecessary. It may make *you* feel better but it may only serve to worry or upset your brother or sister for no good reason.

Recently, a well-meaning lady said to a young mother, 'My conscience has been bothering me since I learned that I must ask forgiveness from anyone that I have been bearing a grudge against or have felt critical about. I want you to forgive me for what I have been thinking about how you are bringing up your children.' She did not expand on this, and left the young woman aghast, crushed and confused. Before the lady had spoken to her, she had not had anything to forgive her for, but now she did have! The lady herself is no doubt now feeling better, but she has selfishly dumped the pain on to the young mother. In cases like this it is better not to let on, but to go directly to God to confess, to forgive and to ask forgiveness.

Prayer

> *Dear Lord,*
>   *Thank you for forgiving me. I confess that I have been bearing a grudge against* ....
> *There is no justification for this even though I have justified it to myself until now.*
>   *I do not want to make excuses any more. Please forgive me. Please show me, too, what I should do and say, and how and when to seek forgiveness from* ....
>   *I pray that we will be reconciled. For Jesus's sake, Amen.*

Action this day

1 Speak or write or phone at least one person whom you have fallen out with (as long as they are aware of the dissension).

   Ask their forgiveness without in any way justifying your behaviour or attitude. Tell them, if appropriate, that you completely forgive them and do not hold it against them any more.
2 Resolve never to let the sun go down on your wrath.

Thoughts for today

- Jesus said, 'And when you stand praying, if you hold anything against anyone, forgive him, so that your Father in heaven may forgive your sins.' (Mark 11:25)
- . . . do not let the sun go down while you are still angry. (Ephesians 4:26)
- Get rid of all bitterness, rage and anger . . . (Ephesians 4:31)
- See to it that no one misses the grace of God and that no bitter root grows up to cause trouble and defile many. (Hebrews 12:15)

Loneliness

The harm – the answer

It is not difficult to see that very severe loneliness can be a big cause of stress. Solitary confinement and the isolation of the Beirut hostages was obviously stressful. How long would Robinson Crusoe have survived if Man Friday had not come along?

But there is today a lot of loneliness, of lesser degree but nevertheless distressing. 'Nobody loves me, nobody cares. Nobody knows how I feel.' Some years ago the extended family was the norm. Grandparents, even great-grandparents sometimes, parents, children – lots of them, and uncles and aunts and cousins all lived together or nearby. Loneliness at that time was less likely. Then families got smaller, and eventually we had the nuclear family: Mum, Dad and 2.4 children. Nowadays single-parent families, the separated, and the old living on their own are becoming increasingly common. More and more are feeling lonely. Many old people living in a room in a home never have any visitors.

To get work, men may have to live away from home during the week or even for longer periods. People work abroad, separated from friends and families – missionaries sometimes for years at a time. Students live away from home and overseas, students in a different culture and climate. Mothers with babies or small children can feel cut off from other adults. When the children grow up and leave home, mothers can feel alone. Bereavement brings loneliness for wives and husbands. Married women can feel lonely when their husbands are at work all day, out at the pub in the evenings, on the golf course or working at weekends.

Men can feel isolated at work, and those who are redundant or retired watch friends and colleagues going to work and feel alone.

You can be lonely in a crowd. Most people now live in towns and cities, surrounded by other people in the building or street, in the supermarket or on the tube, but many are lonely. All degrees and types of loneliness can lead to effects of stress damaging to our health.

Loneliness can predispose to depression. Studies show that it can lower our immunity and therefore our resistance to disease. Medical students who felt lonely were shown to have immunity lower than those who did not. After bereavement immunity is lower, and bereaved spouses are at higher risk of disease and have higher mortality rates.

Why should loneliness cause us such problems? The answer is fairly simple. We have been created as relational beings. John Donne said, 'No man is an island'. Right at the beginning, in Genesis, the Lord God said, 'It is not good for the man to be alone. I will make a helper suitable for him . . . then the Lord God made a woman.' (Genesis 2:18, 22) God designed the family. God meant us to have friends. He meant us to relate and care for and love one another. Remember the story of the Good Samaritan.

Jesus did not live and work and operate on His own. He had a family and a number of friends – and a few very close ones. He also knew what it was like to be lonely and alone. At the end of His earthly life everyone left Him, friends, family, followers. Even those closest to Him, like Peter, rejected Him and said they did not know Him.

People may try different ways of dealing with their loneliness – alcohol, drugs, an affair; they may become addicted to fantasies – soap operas, romantic novels; spend all possible hours immersed in work; take up bad or doubtful company; marry or live together without any love – almost any company is better than being alone and lonely. But with all of these the end results can be worse than the loneliness they were meant to serve.

If we do not, or are not able to, function within relationships, then we will not be functioning as we have been designed to, with possible consequent harm to us.

So for our health's sake, and so that we will be able to withstand pressures, it is important that we do not become or remain lonely, or let it become a habit.

If loneliness has become part of your life, it is not easy to get out of it, but it is possible. Try to avoid the deadly trap of self-pity, as this will only lead to increased feelings of loneliness. It will take an effort, as breaking any habit does, but it will pay rich dividends. The effort needs to come from you, without waiting for other people to make the first approach. Some people always wait for others to take the initiative – 'Nobody spoke to me at the party. Nobody asked how I was. Nobody cares.' But

YOU MUST TAKE THE INITIATIVE

and even more important, when you do

DO NOT BE PUT OFF BY REJECTION.

Some people are afraid of rejection to the extent that they never take any initiative so that they will be spared the rejection. They may even reject or snub others first so that they have pre-empted any rejection which may come.

But remember how in days 11–14 we discovered how God can meet all our longings for relationship. When we are rejected, although we have been hurt, it is no longer devastating, and we can pick ourselves up, dust ourselves off and start all over again, obeying Christ's Law of Love – which is to love others as we have been loved by Christ. The real secret of successful relationships is to enter them not in order to have our own needs met but rather to meet others' needs instead. Our focus is no longer on ourselves, because we have been taken care of by God's love and care, so we can focus on others, seek their highest good rather than our own, and persevere on through the rejections when they come – as they surely will.

One of the best ways of overcoming loneliness is to find someone who is lonely and help and befriend them. You may know someone who is lonely, or you may find them through a voluntary organization or in or through your church.

You may be able to help them in their loneliness and in turn you will be blessed.

Even if you are aware and assured of God's love for you and know that He is always with you, if you have operated for a long time in the above way, then you need to take some positive action to break bad habits. You may have heard that one of the worst things we can do is to tell people who are depressed to 'snap out of it', and in many ways this is true because they cannot just stop feeling depressed. But there does come a time when good advice about being lonely (not just feeling lonely) is to

SNAP OUT OF IT
DO SOMETHING
MAKE AN EFFORT

Do not sit around and mope.

GET UP, GO, DO, SPEAK

and trust God to protect and hold you through the times of rejection.

You need constantly to remember that God has designed things so that you can be part of a large family of brothers and sisters – in the church. So join with other members of your family – meet with them, speak to them, get to know them and ask God how you can be a blessing to them rather than demand that they meet your needs.

*

One word of caution. It is not wise to become totally dependent on others for company and friendship or love. You may lose them. There may be times when all seem to leave you and you really are alone.

BUT YOU ARE NOT TRULY ALONE.
GOD IS WITH YOU

and around you and in you. You can speak to Him, you can be with Him, you can have His company and His love and attention – at any time. Enjoy it, relax in His presence. Give Him time to speak to you. Remember and take hold of the amazing fact that God actually delights in you and eagerly desires your company and relationship and love – that's why He created you in the first place! The Shorter Westminster Catechism states that 'man's chief end is to glorify God AND ENJOY HIM FOR EVER'.

Remember also, you cannot truly love others and enjoy their love until you have received God's love for you. We love because GOD FIRST LOVED US. If the love of God is not real to you, then commit yourself to seek, search and find it through prayer and the power of the Holy Spirit. Believe me, God is totally committed to answering that prayer.

Many people also do not realize that God can fill the emptiness and longing for other human friendships as well as our spiritual longing. We may well be holding an area of our life apart from Him, with the label of 'human friends only' keeping Him out, not believing that this is an area He can deal with too. If this is so, then confess it to God. Repent of keeping it away from Him, admit your longings for friendship to Him, and ask Him to fill that part of your life too.

Prayer

Heavenly Father,

You know that I am (or have been) feeling lonely, You know how it feels because everyone left you when you were here on earth. You know, too, what it is to be rejected, because people are rejecting your love and your approach to them still every day.

Please forgive me for feeling sorry for myself. I want to live as you want me to in relationship with other people. I know that I will have to make an effort to reach out to others and become vulnerable to rejection, and that this may not be easy.

Please help me in this and make it possible for me to meet and become friendly with others.

I know that even if others seem to reject me, you love me and will never leave me, and so although the rejection will hurt, it cannot devastate me. So I WILL trust you and develop our friendship together too. Amen.

Action this day

If you are lonely, decide NOW to do something about it:

1 Make contact with others in your church. Invite them to visit you or offer to visit them.
2 Arrange to join something.
3 Arrange to attend one of your church's meetings this week.
4 Arrange to join a house group in your church.

Thoughts for today

- A father to the fatherless, a defender of widows, is God in his holy dwelling. (Psalm 68:5)
- God sets the lonely in families, he leads forth the prisoners with singing; but the rebellious live in a sun-scorched land. (Psalm 68:6)
- He will never leave you nor forsake you. (Deuteronomy 31:6)
- There is a friend who sticks closer than a brother. (Proverbs 18:24)
- My command is this: Love each other as I have loved you. Greater love has no one than this, that he lay down his life for his friends. (John 15:12, 13)

Day 18

Perfectionism, obsessiveness and compulsiveness

The harm – the answer

It is good to be conscientious, careful and tidy, clean and punctual, and not to be wasteful. Most of these forms of behaviour are reasonable and have a good basis – self-discipline, thoughtfulness and love for others, doing to others as you would have them do to you, thrift – looking after the pennies so that the pounds will look after themselves – looking after your body and its hygiene, being a good and responsible member of society. All of these are seen as virtues and are taught from an early age.

As with so many other things in life, however, there must be

A BALANCE.

If some things get out of hand then problems arise. People can become obsessive and then feel compelled to act in certain ways. Being conscientious can turn into being a perfectionist, being tidy into being house-proud, being tidy and clean into being fastidious or narcissistic, being punctual into being a slave to the clock.

Some of this behaviour, while irritating and a waste of time and energy, is relatively harmless superstition and ritual. As children, we all avoided the lines on the pavement at one time or another. Some sportsmen have to put the right shoe on before the left, or vice versa. Some have to be the last member of the team out of the changing room.

Carried to extremes, however, obsessive behaviour can be very stressful for the one who has to carry it out and to others – spouse, family, friends, colleagues – who have to live with it. It can end up interfering with daily living.

The need to make sure that everything is perfect can actually paralyse. There is so much ritual of planning, discussion and concern that it should be just right that in fact a start is delayed and delayed and may never take place, and what needs to be done is never done. There can be terrible fear that if the ritual is not strictly adhered to, something dire will happen. The rituals may have to be repeated many, many times and started from the beginning again if some small mistake, real or imagined, has been made. A common ritual is washing the hands over and over again before eating or after the slightest soiling, until in the end the skin becomes raw and cracked. Counting everything in sight is another common ritual. The Count in the children's programme 'Sesame Street' has this obsession!

People who get to this stage know that what they are doing is completely irrational but they cannot stop doing it 'just in case'. It's a bit like the story of the man sitting at an open train window blowing peas out of a straw. Intrigued, a fellow passenger asked what he was doing. 'Keeping away the wild elephants', was the reply. 'But there are no wild elephants here!' said the passenger. 'You see how effective it is', said the man.

Neurosis of this kind is obviously worrying and stressful and may need treatment, and may itself be a symptom of underlying anxiety and stress which need treatment.

However, any form of slavery to any obsessions, even harmless ones, can be stressful, and we must be on our guard about this. We should be free to choose what we do and not be compelled from within.

Periodically it is good to examine all you do, and ask yourself, 'Why do I do what I do?' You may be surprised at how much ritual you have fallen into, and how much security you are deriving from it. Today's habits may seem very strange in a few years, whereas at the moment we accept them as important, even essential.

Some of us can remember when all children were given castor oil or syrup of figs every Friday night. Even today in some households food has to be on the table for meals at precise times, indeed to the minute – a few minutes late and Dad or Grandad are irritated for the rest of the day.

It's not too long ago since children – especially in Scotland – were not allowed to whistle on Sundays, let alone kick a ball or have a game of tennis. In some church services there has to be a set number of hymns and prayers, in a certain order. In others there has to be a prescribed period for singing songs, repeated a certain number of times. Some have to attend church twice on a Sunday – morning and evening.

There is often no medical or logical or even biblical reason for what we felt or feel we HAVE to do.

Children are not unhealthy because the Friday night 'opener' ritual has been dropped, or because tonsils are not taken out so much nowadays. Stomachs and bodies will not starve or be harmed if meals are sometimes earlier, or sometimes later than usual.

Jesus Himself said that the Sabbath was made for man and not man for the Sabbath. While we believe that Sundays should be the Lord's Day, a day of rest with as few distractions as possible, it is not healthy for us to become stressed because of our man-made rules and traditions. Almost certainly others, just as well-meaning and pious, will have different, even contradictory, ones. In Eastern Europe, Christian women will not wear jewellery, but the men will smoke cigarettes freely. In some churches hats are *de rigueur* while in others few will be seen.

We should, and should want to, worship God and meet with fellow believers, His people, our brothers and sisters, on Sundays, but there is nothing in the Bible to say that this must be twice on a Sunday or at a set time.

Often what is happening is that we are depending upon these rituals and traditions to give us a sense of security rather than on God Himself, and this is not pleasing to God. Christ died to set us free from bondage to things of the world, to make us feel safe, worthwhile and significant, so Christians have no business continuing to behave as if we had not been set free. If Christ has set us free, then we are free indeed. We will be loved and secure whether or not we do any of these things, and that is the way God wants it to be. Our security is now an inner security, not an outer scaffolding, which we have to strive to keep in place and defend.

So it is important that our behaviour reflects the truth of our inner security. Self-discipline is good, even to the point of sometimes disciplining ourselves not to be too disciplined or rigid.

Relax, smile; loosen up in mind and body and behaviour. It will not be the end, or 'awful' if something is not done perfectly or even if it is not done at all.

Prayer

Heavenly Father,
   Please forgive me for being a slave to ....
Show me when it is important to do things and to do them in a certain way. Show me when I am merely following ritual or habit and stressing myself because of this or wasting valuable time.
   Thank you for the freedom and security we have in the Lord Jesus and please help me to free myself from all things and habits which bind me. In Jesus's name, Amen.

Action this day

1 Take something you do regularly or some habit you have. Examine it. Ask yourself why you do it. Is it necessary or good for you or others? Are you doing it the best way? Is the time you take doing it well spent?
2 Stop doing one thing today which is unnecessary, and not useful or helpful to yourself or others – constantly reminding yourself that it is God you trust not this ritual or habit, and that it will not be 'awful' if you don't do it.
3 Change the way you do something today. For example – walk a different way to work, take a different bus, sit in a different seat; have a meal at a different time – BREAK THE MOULD!

Thoughts for today

- It is for freedom that Christ has set us free. (Galatians 5:1)
- For in Christ Jesus neither circumcision nor uncircumcision has any value. (Galatians 5:6)
- Jesus said, 'Then you will know the truth, and the truth will set you free.' (John 8:32)
- So if the Son sets you free, you will be free indeed. (John 8:36)
- Everything is permissible – but not everything is beneficial. Everything is permissible – but not everything is constructive. Nobody should seek his own good, but the good of others. (1 Corinthians 10:23, 24)
- You foolish Galatians! Who has bewitched you? . . . After beginning with the Spirit, are you now trying to attain your goal by human effort? (Galatians 3:1, 3)

Day 19

It's good to have goals –
if they're good goals!

In this life it is good to have goals; something to work for, strive for or practise for. When we attain our goal, it is satisfying, gives us a sense of achievement, especially if it has stretched us, and does wonders for our self-esteem.

However, if we do not succeed or achieve our goal, or if we have set our hearts on something and it does not happen, we can become disappointed, then frustrated and dejected and even depressed. We may begin to worry about it, try harder to achieve or make it happen, get anxious and eventually suffer from effects of stress.

It is important therefore that goals in life do stretch us a bit but are within our reach so that we have a good chance of achieving them. It is also important that they are fairly specific so that we are clear when we have reached them. Thus the actual setting of goals is of paramount importance.

It may help you to remember that they should be 'RATED'.

'R' = *Realistic*
It can almost go without saying that our goals should be realistic and that we should be able to recognize our limitations and abilities. To set out to be a champion highjumper when we are only 5′4″ tall is likely to end in failure and ignominy.

'A' = *Achievable*
Our goals should not only be realistic but there should be a reasonable chance of achieving them.

'T' = *Tax*

At the same time they should tax and stretch us so that there is a real sense of achievement when we succeed. They should not be set so low that little effort is required.

'E' = *Evaluable*

We should set clear goals which have an end point so that we know when we have achieved them. If we make our goal 'To become a better golfer' this is too woolly. When are we going to be satisfied that we have become better?

A better and more specific goal which we can 'evaluate' and know when we have achieved it would be 'To get my handicap down to "x" strokes.' Better still, put a time on it and then evaluate it at the end of the time: 'To get my handicap down to "x" strokes by June next year.'

Most goals which entail 'improving' or 'getting better at' are best translated into more concrete terms which we can measure and know they have been achieved in a certain time.

'D' = *Dependent*

Ideally our goals should be achievable through our own efforts. If an outcome depends on other people or circumstances then we are not in control. We run the risk of non-achievement, with all that entails, through no fault of our own.

So when we are setting ourselves goals we should make sure that they are

'RATED'.

But – what about goals that are set for us?

By a boss – 'Finish these tasks quickly.'
By a sport – 'Improve before you can go on to higher levels
of competition.'
By a spouse – 'Become better, more loving, more caring, more
understanding.'
By a parent – 'Become more obedient.'
'Improve your behaviour.'

> By a church – 'Attend more; pray more; give more; take part more.'

If possible, we should try to discuss and negotiate 'RATED' goals in all situations. Unfortunately others are not always as willing to set 'RATED' goals for us, as we are for ourselves. If our negotiation fails then we must realize that the goals we have been set may not be achieved in the eyes of the one who set them. We may not even know that we have achieved them.

If really important issues are at stake, we may have to make a stand and decline to accept the goals in this form. This, of course, may have consequences for our job, our career, our marriage or our family so it must not be done lightly. However, it may be the only wise decision at this stage, to save much greater problems for our life later.

In our enthusiasm to set goals (prayerfully), there is a danger that we will set too many. It is best not to have too many and we suggest that you start with one or two, or at least no more than one in each area of your life – at work, in family life, church life, personal life – and seek out the mind of Christ as to what those goals should be for you.

Prayer

Heavenly Father,

I can see the importance of setting goals in my life, and with your help, I mean to do this. Please show me those areas that need goals at this time. Give me wisdom to know your mind for me, and enable me to set your 'Rated' goals in these areas. Please then give me the ability and impetus to reach these goals through the power of your Holy Spirit. For Jesus's sake, Amen.

Action this day

1 Having prayed as above, decide which areas of your life need goals now.
2 Set goals for these areas. Make sure they are 'RATED'. Write them down.
3 Put an entry in your diary on the date that each goal should be reviewed and assessed as to outcome.
4 Are there any goals being set for you by others at this time? Consider discussing and 'negotiating' these with whoever has or is setting you goals – in order to get them 'RATED' – and then do them as unto the Lord.

Thoughts for today

- But one thing I do: Forgetting what is behind, and straining towards what is ahead, I press on towards the goal to win the prize for which God has called me heavenwards in Christ Jesus. (Philippians 3:13,14)
- So we make it our goal to please Him, whether we are at home in the body or away from it. For we must all appear before the judgement seat of Christ, that each one may receive what is due to him for the things done while in the body, whether good or bad. (2 Corinthians 5:9, 10)

Day 20

How to be always a winner – never a loser

We saw yesterday that it is good to set ourselves goals. We also saw that achieving our goals makes us feel good. Failure to achieve can lead to effects of stress.

We saw that we should set ourselves 'RATED' goals (Realistic, Achievable, Taxing, Evaluable, and where achieving them does not Depend on others). We suggested that if we are set goals by someone else we should try to negotiate so that they will be 'RATED'.

HOWEVER, there are two very important areas when goals cannot be fully 'RATED' – a far as the 'D' is concerned, i.e. where the outcome is not entirely under our control – and thus we are dependent on others, or on circumstances for their achievement. This will not matter IF THE GOAL IS ACHIEVED. But if it is not achieved then we have a problem. Not only will we be disappointed and perhaps stressed, but since it is not under our control, we may become very frustrated, anxious and even more stressed.

Let's look at these two areas and see what you can do to prevent yourself getting into this stressed situation.

1 This is when you decide to accept from another goals which you cannot completely control.

For example, when a school teacher accepts that his or her goal is to get a certain pass rate for the class. If achieved, he or she feels good. But in the end, the pass rate will depend on a number of factors, the pupils themselves, the exam itself, the pass mark set and so on – all of them outside the control of the teacher. Failure can bring stress.

Or when a police officer accepts a goal of getting a conviction in court. If he gets it, he has succeeded, but in the end his success or failure is in the hands of the magistrate, or judge or jury. Failure can bring stress.

Or when a football manager accepts a goal of winning the cup, or getting into the premier division. His success or failure depends much on his players and on other teams, sometimes on referees' decisions. If he succeeds – great! If he fails – stress!

Or when a salesperson accepts a goal of a certain sales target. In the end he depends on others to buy. Success is not in his own hands. Failure can bring anxiety and stress.

2 The other big area where goals cannot be 'RATED' is when you have a VISION, but its realization depends on others apart from yourself.

For example, at work your vision may be to become head of the department, or head of the firm. If you make it – good. However, no matter how hard you work, you may be passed over. The final decision about promotion does not lie with you but with others, and failure may lead to stress.

At home, your vision may be that your children will do well at school. You can get as far as 'RATE' with this but the 'D' is not available to you. **You** cannot ensure that they do well. To a large extent it is up to them, to the teachers, to the system. If they do well, you are elated. If they do not you can become very dejected, try even harder to push them to do well, and eventually end up in disappointment. Anxiety, depression and effects of stress may follow.

In the family your vision may be that your husband or wife becomes a Christian like you. You may go to extremes in trying to get this to happen – praying, leaving books and texts about the place for him or her to find, suggesting books they read, giving invitations to church or special meetings, arranging 'accidental' meetings with other Christians – all to no avail.

We heard of one lady who did all this and more. Everywhere her husband turned he was faced by a text – above the shaving mirror: 'You must be born again'; on the inside of the fridge door: 'I am the way, the truth and the life.' Even when he lay down in bed at night there was one on the ceiling that read 'Nothing is impossible with God'! Unfortunately it may have been completely misconstrued by a visiting missionary couple who were given their room, and who asked our lady friend the next morning if she would like prayer for her marriage!

All your efforts to convert your wife or husband may come to naught, in fact all you may succeed in doing is to make them more resistant. This is followed by you redoubling your efforts, more resistance, more disappointment, and eventually frustration and depression for you. Their conversion is not under your control.

What is the answer to save you from unnecessary stress in these two situations?

Firstly – this should not put you off keeping the goal given you by others very clearly in your mind as *what you should aim at*. Similarly, it should not put you off having a *vision*, something you dream of and keep alive in your mind and life. You should pray for success in the goals given to you and for your vision to become a reality.

Secondly, if you are going to avoid possible effects of stress, you must realize that goals given to you by other people, and often your own vision, are not completely under your control. You will have to depend on others for their outcome.

YOU SHOULD NOT TAKE RESPONSIBILITY FOR THEIR OUTCOME. ULTIMATELY, THAT IS IN GOD'S HANDS. HE IS ULTIMATELY RESPONSIBLE.

Instead, you should take responsibility for WHAT *YOU* DO AND HOW YOU DO IT. YOUR GOALS should be:

a) to DO YOUR BEST, at work, in the house, as a parent, as a wife/husband, in your church relationship and work.

b) to DO WHAT IS RIGHT – no compromises, no fudging the issues; and most important of all

c) to GLORIFY AND PLEASE GOD in all your words and actions. You are responsible for understanding and learning what will please Him in any given circumstances, through searching His book and learning from other mature Christians.

All of these are within your control and it is up to you whether you succeed in them or not. If you make these your goals and not the outcome – leaving that to God – then

YOU CAN ALWAYS BE A WINNER.

You need never be desperately frustrated or dejected or anxious or depressed again.

YOU NEED NEVER FAIL.

The other side of the coin is this. When you feel frustrated, anxious, depressed or stressed in any situation or relationship or circumstance it may well be because your goal is not being achieved. You have to ask whether you have made yourself responsible for the wrong goal – the outcome rather than

DOING YOUR BEST
DOING WHAT IS RIGHT
PLEASING GOD.

If you have, then you must drop the outcome goal, decide there and then that your only goal will be these three. The negative feelings should then melt away because you know you can succeed in your real goals.

Prayer

Heavenly Father,
   I can see that there are many things in life which are not under my control. Help me not to take responsibility for them but to take responsibility for above all glorifying and pleasing you. I can decide then what to do with your help and can always be a winner and a success in your eyes. Thank you Father, Amen.

Action this day

1 Examine the main areas of your life. What are your goals or visions for these areas? Are you in ultimate control of their achievement?

2 Where you are not – determine from now on that your only goals will be

   TO DO YOUR BEST
   TO DO WHAT'S RIGHT
   TO DO WHAT WILL GLORIFY AND PLEASE GOD.

3 In each area, think, pray and search the Bible for what your actions should be, so that you will please God by them. (If you have a concordance you can look up these areas and then study the relevant Bible texts and passages.)

Thoughts for today

- Jesus said, 'But seek first His kingdom, and His righteousness, and these things will be given to you as well.' (Matthew 6:33)
- So whatever you eat or drink or whatever you do, do it all for the glory of God. (1 Corinthians 10:31)
- and find out what pleases the Lord. (Ephesians 5:10)
- Therefore do not be foolish, but understand what the Lord's will is. (Ephesians 5:17)

- Now listen, you who say, 'Today or tomorrow we will go to this or that city, spend a year there, carry on business and make money.' Why you do not even know what will happen tomorrow . . . Instead, you ought to say, 'If it is the Lord's will, we will live and do this or that.' . . . Anyone, then, who knows the good he ought to do and doesn't do it, sins. (James 4:13–17)

- Obey them [masters] not only to win their favour when their eye is on you, but like slaves of Christ, doing the will of God from your heart. Serve wholeheartedly, as if you were serving the Lord, not me, because you know that the Lord will reward everyone for whatever good he does, whether he is slave or free. (Ephesians 6:7, 8)

Problems and pressures – the first step

So far we have not mentioned or dealt with problems, and this has been on purpose.

However, if you have been practising the relaxation exercises regularly, and if you have dealt with and are dealing with the general issues we have raised, then you now are in a position to set about dealing with specific pressures and problems in your life.

Some people try to ignore these, hoping they will go away. Instead of disappearing, however, they can keep on growing, and can become much more troublesome and more difficult to deal with in the end. Small debts, if ignored, can continue to grow and eventually get out of hand. Even though, by ignoring problems, you forget about them sometimes, they may continue to rumble away in your subconscious, slowly eroding your peace of mind and your health.

Others try to run away from problems – only to find that the problems have a tendency to follow them or are replaced by others in the new situation.

But a ship in a storm does best if it faces into the storm.

So step 1 is . . .

Take a good hard look at all the problems and pressures in your life. Write each one down, a new page to each. Below the problem, write down what it is that worries and bothers you about it, what really gets to you and bugs you. Be honest and open – after all, nobody need see what you have written.

The very fact that you have faced up to the problems and put them down on paper will bring a measure of release.

Recently a study showed that by writing about their fears and worries the immunity and health of a group of students improved considerably. Those who wrote about things they had never before confided to anyone, had the biggest rise in immunity.

Step 2

It can help even more if you tell someone else about these problems. So, if you have an understanding spouse or relation or good friend or counsellor that you can open up to then

SHARE YOUR PROBLEMS

with them – NOT at this time to ask for advice but simply to voice your concerns and fears to them.

Step 3

Although we said that no one need read what you have written, and you may not have anyone you feel you can confide in – there is one who already knows: God Himself. He is longing to help you with your worries and problems and to care for you. It is wonderful to know that, even though He is the God of the universe, He cares – about your big pressures, and the little ones.

We were at a Christian meeting recently where the speaker was talking about God's care. 'Even the hairs of your head are numbered,' he said – and then as an aside he blurted out spontaneously, but not irreverently, 'What a waste of time!' At the coffee break, a young man in a cap came up to the speaker and said, 'It has meant so much recently to know that God knows and cares so much about me – that He knows the number of hairs on my head.' Taking off his cap he said, 'You see, recently I was diagnosed as having cancer. I have had to have radiotherapy and chemotherapy, and all my hair fell out. But now it's beginning to grow back and it reminds me daily that God knows about me and cares and loves me, and I am so grateful. It means so much to me.'

So we suggest you offer up the pages you have written to Him as you say this prayer.

Prayer

Heavenly Father,
You know all about me. You know about the pressures in my life and you know what really worries me. You have seen what I have written down and know what is in my heart. I now confess to you that I have these problems and worries and I place them in your hands – in Jesus's name. Amen.

Thoughts for today

- Therefore confess your sins to each other and pray for each other so that you may be healed. (James 5:16)
- Cast all your cares on Him for He cares for you. (1 Peter 5:7)
- And even the very hairs on your head are all numbered. (Matthew 10:30)

Dealing with problems and pressures

Whether you actually yet feel different or not, we promise that because of what you wrote and prayed yesterday, your body and mind is now freer and healthier than before you started to write. Your immunity will have been boosted and *health-giving chemicals will be at work in your body and brain*. You will begin to experience the benefits over the coming days and weeks.

BUT THERE'S MORE.

Go back to the pages you wrote yesterday. Divide them into two piles (we're assuming that you have quite a few!).

Pile (1) – those problems and pressures that have come upon you or have built up in your life through no fault of your own. We will deal with these tomorrow.

Pile (2) – those that, at least in part, you have brought on yourself either wittingly or unwittingly. You will have to be really honest about this. It is not easy to admit, even to yourself, that some of your problems are self-inflicted. Look again at pile (1) – are there any there, if you are being absolutely honest, you should move to pile (2)? – then move them.

Now look separately at each problem in pile (2). Is there anything *you* can do either to get rid of or reduce these pressures?

It may be difficult for you to see how it is going to be done, but don't let this put you off at this stage. Make a start, think of possibilities. It may be necessary for you to call on one of the sources of support you identified on day 6.

Is the problem financial? Can you reduce expenditure in any way? Can you increase income in any way? Can you budget better?

Quite drastic means may be needed. But before taking any action, consider getting sound and trustworthy advice.

Have you been less than honest in any way, with a continuing fear that you may be found out? Decide how best to rectify things.

Have you taken on too many commitments, so that your schedule is now so heavy that life is a burden and a rush and a worry, rather than each day being relished and enjoyed? What should go?

A number of years ago, every evening Bill drove frantically home after a long and tiring day's work, so that he could snatch a quick meal before rushing out to chair a committee meeting at the golf club, the Rotary Club, the school governors, the medical association, St John's Ambulance, St Andrew's Society. Every evening there was something.

One evening as he raced home it all suddenly came home to him. He was in a frenetic rush of his own making, wearing himself out, with no time to relax and really enjoy himself and the family. On the spur of the moment he decided to resign from everything. Impulsive? Yes, but probably life-saving.

It took some time to adjust. His body and brain had to get used to being able to relax. They often shrieked for their adrenalin 'fix'. Then he slowly began to enjoy it. But then came times when he felt bored. Slowly, and this time thoughtfully, and after due consideration, he decided what to take up again – still leaving time to relax.

Perhaps this was a drastic way of doing things and not necessary for you, at this time. But it might be good to

TAKE A SABBATICAL

from one or two of the many things you are involved in. Give yourself time to work out which are the really important ones to keep on and how many activities you should end up doing on a continuing basis.

Have you agreed to, or set yourself, unrealistic deadlines? (I await the shout from Frances as she types this bit!) Every piece of writing I do I am far too optimistic about when it can be ready, and then the pressure starts to build. How can I possibly manage it? What can I drop? How can I make more time? Often the only answer is to reset the deadline. What a relief when I do bring myself to do this, with a tacit admission and confession that I am not as quick or as efficient as I had made out to be.

Are you needing to renegotiate any deadlines with others or with yourself? Better of course to be realistic in the first place.

Have you cut yourself off from family or friends? Do you need to make contact to re-establish links?

Do you have a drink, or drugs or eating or health problem? Do you need to seek professional advice or take other first steps on the road to recovery?

Is there some sin which you know should not be in your life?

There may be other problems in your life which are self-inflicted. You need to examine them and see what you can do about them. Whatever it is

SEEK ADVICE
DECIDE WHAT HAS TO BE DONE
DO IT.

This itself will release the tension even before any other results of your actions take place or the problem is solved. But tension will remain and even increase if you decide what needs to be done but do nothing about it.

So, DECIDE AND DO.

Prayer

Dear Father,
I confess that some of my pressures are self-inflicted. Please forgive me and show me if there are others which I have brought on myself. Please help me now, as I decide to rectify matters. Give me the courage and commitment to do what needs to be done. In Jesus's name, Amen.

Action this day

1 Decide which pressures AT THIS TIME you have inflicted on yourself. Be honest. Go over pile (1) again – should any more be moved to pile (2)?
2 Arrange to discuss these with a trusted confidante with a view to doing what needs to be done about these pressures.
3 When you have decided what needs to be done MAKE A START ON DOING IT.

Thoughts for today

- The heart is deceitful above all things. (Jeremiah 17:9)
- Let us throw off everything that hinders and the sin that so easily entangles, and let us run with perseverance the race marked out for us. (Hebrews 12:1)
- For the Lord gives wisdom, and from His mouth comes knowledge and understanding. (Proverbs 2:6)

Day 23

More about dealing with problems and pressures

We have seen that facing up to pressures and problems, writing them down and talking them over can be of great benefit to us physically, emotionally and mentally.

Yesterday we went a step further. We hope that you will, by now, have started to deal with self-inflicted pressures in your life – those which, to some extent, you brought on yourself and therefore have some control over. If you have made a start the chemicals associated with tension, anxiety and fear will have begun to change and this will in time benefit your body and brain.

But many of us struggle with pressures that we have not brought on ourselves. We have responsibilities and we cannot ignore or relinquish these. What about this kind of problem? Looking after a handicapped child, ageing parents, a disabled husband or wife; coping with chronic illness, a difficult boss, difficult colleagues, a stressful job; responsibilities at home, at work, in our church; unemployment. There may be others in pile (1) which you made yesterday.

The first thing to do is to accept that these circumstances exist. They do cause pressure. They will not go away, at least not in the foreseeable future. So, unlike many of the self-inflicted pressures, you cannot discard them and you will have to live with them.

If they are intractable and serious problems then they may get you down at least part of the time. You may even feel helpless and hopeless and have come to believe that nothing can be done about them.

But perhaps all is not lost. There may be actions you can take to lessen the pressures they cause. We recommend you take a few well tried steps in

PROBLEM SOLVING

applying these steps to each problem in pile (1).

Step 1

Ask yourself what exactly is the problem. You may have already got part of the way when you originally wrote it down. But it's *not enough* to say

'My difficult teenager'
'My difficult parents'
'My stressful job'
'My impossible boss'.

If you leave the problem as big and 'global' and vague as this, then there can only be a big global solution –

put the teenager out;
abandon your parents;
leave your job;
shoot your boss.

But you cannot and must not contemplate such a global solution (at least not as a first choice!).

Try to ask yourself more precisely, 'What is my problem?' Try to break it down, to analyse it a bit. What exactly is it about my difficult teenager, my parents, my job, my boss that causes the pressure? Is it the rows with my teenager? His or her untidiness? thoughtlessness? noise? friends? – or what? And how do these pressure and exasperate me?

Is it the demandingness of my parents? their interference? the physical effort of looking after them? or what? and so on.

Step 2

Ask yourself, 'What do I want to accomplish by solving the problem?'
  – more rest? more peace? less aggro? more time to myself? more satisfaction? – or what?

Step 3

What can you do to accomplish the aim(s) of (2)? Look at all the possibilities. Never mind *at this stage* whether they are feasible or possible. Put them all down.

Step 4

What might happen if you adopt the best of these solutions?

Step 5

What have you decided to do?

Step 6

Go over in your mind, or possibly with a friend, what you will say and how you will do it. Imagine yourself saying and doing it. Imagine the consequences. (When they do happen – they will not be as bad or affect you as badly if you have 'rehearsed' them in this way.)

Step 7

DO IT! You may be surprised at how easy it is and how you succeed. BUT do not be put off by a failure.

Step 8

Ask yourself, 'How did it go? Could I do better? Can I do it again? Could I do it differently?'

It can be of tremendous help to enlist the help of your spouse or a trusted friend as you work through each step for each of the troubles or pressures on each page in pile (1).

Postscript

With some pressures, sometimes, in some cases, and usually as a last resort, it may be necessary and wise to

LEAVE, CHANGE, MOVE.

It may be the only thing left, and the only thing to do – in the end.

BUT – if you do decide to take such a drastic step – first take every possible precaution that you do not go from the frying pan into the fire.

A few years ago you might have decided to 'get away from it all' and have gone off to a quiet island in the South Atlantic, only to find that the Argentines and then the British were fighting over your home – in the Falklands!

Prayer

Heavenly Father,
   You know that I am under great pressure from ....
Please help me to break this problem down. Show me what
the real sources of pressure are. Please guide me as to how I
should deal with this. Please give me courage and wisdom as I
decide and put into effect what seem to be the best actions to
take at this time. In Jesus's name, I ask it. Amen.

Action this day

1 Work through one of your pressures using the problem-solving steps you have learned.
2 Act to bring about a solution to one part at least of this pressure.
3 Make plans to work through the other pressures in pile (1).

Thoughts for today

- If any of you lacks wisdom, he should ask God, who gives generously to all without finding fault, and it will be given to him. (James 1:5)
- Make plans by seeking advice; if you wage war, obtain guidance. (Proverbs 20:18)
- You guide me with your counsel. (Psalm 73:24)

Where do negative feelings come from?

Our feelings and emotions seem to produce or go with certain chemicals and hormones which affect our body cells and either benefit them or harm them, producing illnesses or disease.

Negative feelings like undue anxiety or bitterness are associated with chemicals which can harm our body, whereas feelings of exhilaration or peace and calm are good for our bodies because of the chemicals associated with them.

It is important therefore that our feelings are 'good' for as much of the time as possible. But can we control our feelings? Difficult! If we are feeling afraid and anxious we can try to change the feelings, but will probably not be too successful and the feelings will continue.

HOWEVER, IT IS POSSIBLE TO CONTROL AND
CHANGE OUR FEELINGS

in a different way. But first, we must understand a few things about them.

Have you ever thought what actually produces our feelings? At first sight it would seem to be the circumstances we are in or the things that have happened or are happening to us – at work, at home or in our families.

For example, the sequence seems to go something like:

EVENT→	FEELINGS→	CHEMICALS→	RESULT
Promotion→ at work	Feelings of→ elation and achievement	'good' chemical→ hormonal changes	increase in energy and well being

BUT

For someone else, the sequence might be:

Promotion→ at work	Feelings of→ fear and inadequacy	'bad' chemical→ hormonal changes	anxiety, head- aches lack of energy

Why the difference? The difference in feelings came about as a result of how person (a) and person (b) saw or interpreted the event of promotion. Person (a) saw promotion as a just reward for his work, a recognition of his abilities, a chance to prove how good he is and the opportunity to go on to greater things. Person (b), on the other hand, wondered how he would get on with the demands of the new job, saw himself not being able to cope, having to struggle constantly to prove that he had been worthy of the promotion, probably having to work longer hours to keep up. The sequence really is:

Promotion→Thinking→feelings→chemical changes→effects
or interpretation hormonal changes and
of the event behaviour

In other words, it is not the EVENT of promotion which gave rise to the feelings or to the chemicals or the result in the body, but how person (a) and person (b) interpreted or saw promotion.

So, what we think about things, how we interpret them, and

what we believe about them is more important for our peace of mind and health than what actually happens to us.

You remember the story of David and Goliath? David, facing the giant, might have thought, 'This fellow is so big, I shall never be able to beat him', and he would then have felt afraid, and might have run away, which is what the Israelites thought and felt and were wanting to do.

Or David could have thought, 'This fellow is so big, I really will not be able to miss!' so he felt confident and bravely stood his ground and fired off his sling, killing Goliath. David's feelings depended on how he saw things.

Do you find it difficult to have a quiet time daily with God? You don't really look forward to it and don't feel that you enjoy it, may even feel bored? Would you like to feel excited about it, have a burning desire to give up time for it – to feel that you can't wait till it's time to sit down for it? You can feel like that. Here's how.

If your thinking became something like 'In the next fifteen minutes I will have an audience with the King of kings, my creator, the creator of the universe. I will have His undivided attention for that period. I will be able to speak to Him, say whatever I want and He will speak to me, accept me, welcome me, delight in me and love me. What a sensation, what a thrill, what an honour, what a privilege!' Then your quiet time will change dramatically. You will feel unable to wait till it's time for it, will not want to miss it for anything, and you will want to prolong it rather than cutting it down in time.

Your thinking about your quiet time will have determined your feelings about it

AND YOUR BEHAVIOUR!

Note one more important thing. Most of the people who come to us for counselling, most people who are anxious or depressed, want their feelings changed – very understandably. But, if the feelings are really the result of how they have been thinking, or seeing things, or interpreting them, it is important that we try to change not their feelings but the thinking which has caused the feelings in the first place.

If a bad skin rash is due to a blood disorder, you would not be wise or be too successful if you treat only the skin rather than the underlying disease. A lotion for the skin might temporarily soothe it but if the underlying cause is not dealt with the rash will reappear very quickly.

Many churches nowadays have a 'ministry' time during the Sunday services when people are invited to come out for prayer for healing or guidance or other problems. Often they say they feel anxious or afraid, or depressed. They would like to feel calm: 'Please will you pray for peace for me?' If they are prayed for, simply, like that, God, in His grace, may touch them and then, almost at once, they may feel better and have a large measure of peace.

However, if when they leave church all the worried, anxious thoughts, which gave rise to the lack of peace in the first place, come back, then as sure as eggs is eggs, the feelings of peace will evaporate and the feelings of anxiety return. We need to help them to deal with the worrying thoughts which have been producing the anxious feelings.

Prayer

Heavenly Father,

Please show me the importance of how I see and interpret things, because I can understand now that how I do will greatly influence my feelings, my body chemistry and my health.

Help me to look beyond my feelings and show me the thinking and beliefs which are at the root of my anxieties. For Jesus's sake, Amen.

Action this day

1 Go over a recent event which has caused a lot of pressure in your life. How did you FEEL about it? (anxious, worried, fearful, panicky, tense, angry, resentful, hurt, guilty, ashamed, etc.) Now try to work out and write down the way you saw things and what your inner thoughts must have been (even though you might not have expressed them at the time).

2 Take something that happens to you today. Try to work out the THINKING that goes on in your head about it. How did you FEEL about it? What happens to your feelings if you change your thinking?

Thoughts for today

- There is nothing either good or bad, but thinking makes it so. (Shakespeare)
- A cheerful heart is good medicine. (Proverbs 17:22)
- How long must I wrestle with my thoughts and every day have sorrow in my heart? (Psalm 13:2)

How to deal with negative feelings

We saw yesterday that our feelings have a major impact on our body chemistry and in turn on our health. It is of great importance, therefore, that our feelings are positive for as much of the time as possible.

But it is very difficult for us to change our feelings. We can say, 'I'm not going to feel anxious' or 'I'm going to stop feeling depressed' – but it is unlikely that our feelings will change. We will still go on feeling anxious or depressed.

However, we also saw yesterday, our feelings about events are usually determined by our thinking or belief about those events or our interpretation of them – how we 'see' them – and so to change our feelings we shall have to change our thinking. It also follows that

IF OUR THINKING/BELIEF/INTERPRETATION is FAULTY then OUR FEELINGS WILL BE FAULTY

and the actions that follow will also be faulty or inappropriate.

EVENT→ FAULTY→   FAULTY→ FAULTY
        INTERPRETATION FEELINGS BEHAVIOUR

Let us take an example from the Bible. When the children of Israel got out of Egypt and were in the wilderness, Moses sent twelve men to explore and spy on Canaan – the 'promised land' (see Numbers 13 and 14). When they returned, ten of them reported:

the land does flow with milk and honey . . . But the people are powerful, and the cities are fortified and very large . . . the land devours those living in it. All the people we saw there are of great size. We saw the Nephilim there . . . We seemed like grasshoppers in our own eyes, and we looked the same to them.

So the people all felt afraid and anxious, and stayed where they were, taking no action to enter the promised land. However, two of the spies – Joshua and Caleb, who had seen the same things as the other ten – interpreted it all differently. They reported back:

The land is very good . . . The Lord will lead us into that land and will give it to us . . . Their protection is gone . . . Do not be afraid of them . . . We should go up and take possession of the land, for we can easily do it.

It is important for us to note that both the ten and the two saw exactly the same things but they interpreted them differently – their thinking and their beliefs were different. One interpretation led to feelings of anxiety, a desire to return to Egypt and to actions which kept them in the wilderness for a very long time. The other interpretation and the belief that God would go with them and give them the country led to feelings of confidence, and would have led on to action, of going in and taking the land – if the people had agreed with them.

In shorthand: the ten saw giants and Joshua and Caleb saw giant grapes. We know that the interpretation of the ten was faulty, giving rise to faulty (negative) feelings and to faulty actions and behaviour.

A friend of ours, Ian Barclay, tells of two soldier friends who had undergone ten weeks of gruelling and exhausting training prior to possible promotion. On the last day of the course they were told that they could have the evening off to go into town and enjoy themselves. This involved a ferry trip, and they were told that the last ferry to get them back to base in time was at ten o'clock. Anyone not getting back in time would have to repeat the whole ten-week course.

No way did they want to go through all that again, so no matter what, our two friends determined to be back on the last ferry. They had a wonderful evening out and were on their way back when, as they came over the brow of the hill, horror of horrors – they saw the last ferry several feet out from the jetty. Not just anxiety, but sheer panic seized them. They took off like a bullet from a gun. Adrenalin surging, they might well have beaten the Olympic hundred metres record – and then with a last great effort they hurled themselves out over the water. Jesse Owens or Carl Lewis might have been more elegant but we doubt if they would have jumped further! They positively soared through the air with feet outstretched in front of them.

Both landed in a heap on the deck. A cheer went up from the other passengers. 'Made it!' they breathed in relief as they got up and dusted themselves off. It was only then they realized that the ferry was coming in, not going out. A funny story which, however, illustrates important points about our thinking, feelings and behaviour.

Our two friends' perception of the ferry caused the feelings of panic and anxiety. This in turn gave rise to their actions – the mad run and dangerous jump from the quayside. But their interpretation was faulty – they had misinterpreted things – and so their fears and anxieties, the surges of adrenalin and how they behaved, were totally unnecessary and 'faulty'. If they had interpreted the situation correctly, then those feelings and behaviours would have been entirely different and would have been 'correct'.

How do you tend to look on things that are happening, or have happened, to you? Do you usually see the black side – like the ten spies, or do you tend to see the silver lining, or are you realistic, seeing both good and bad in each situation?

How you usually 'see' things will determine the kind of feelings which will follow, and in turn the effect on your brain and body, and probably your actions and behaviour too.

Has some of your recent thinking and interpretation of events really been a bit off-beam? – like the soldiers and the ferry – faulty and exaggerated, very emotional, completely pessimistic? If it has, then you may well have been experiencing feelings of anxiety, depression, even hopelessness, and you may have been acting and behaving accordingly.

One other imporant point: At any time

IF YOU HAVE NEGATIVE FEELINGS – ANXIETY, FEAR, DEPRESSION HOPELESSNESS – IT IS WISE TO EXAMINE YOUR THINKING.

What thinking went on to produce the feelings? Was it 'good', 'correct', 'appropriate' thinking – or was it 'faulty' in some way? If the thinking has been faulty then the feelings you have been experiencing have been 'faulty' – and unnecessary.

ALL THIS IS VERY IMPORTANT

because, while you cannot change your feelings, you can begin to change the 'faults' in your thinking and in this way

CONTROL YOUR FEELINGS.

Prayer

Lord Jesus,
I can see that often I feel anxious and depressed because of the way I have been seeing and interpreting things.
I am beginning to see that often I see things 'wrongly'. Please show me where my thinking about and interpretation of events has been faulty and what has been wrong with it.
Please help me to see things and think about them more realistically, and to interpret them as they really are, so that my feelings will become more positive. Amen.

Action this day

1 Take an event in your life which has caused a lot of pressure.
2 How have you FELT about it?
3 Try to 'analyse' your thinking about it.
4 Then ask yourself – was your thinking accurate? exaggerated? too pessimistic? where was it 'faulty'? (If you find it difficult to do this on your own, ask a trusted friend to do it with you.)

Thoughts for today

- We take captive every thought to make it obedient to Christ. (2 Corinthians 10:5)

How to change negative feelings to positive ones

Let us recap where we've got to with this important subject of feelings.

1. The sequence goes something like:

Event→thinking→ 'good' feelings→ 'good' chemicals→ body
              or   'good' behaviour   built up
         'bad' feelings→ 'bad' chemicals→ body
                          'bad' behaviour   potentially
                                           damaged

2

Event→'faulty' thinking→ faulty→ bad chemicals→ unnecessary
     and interpretation feelings faulty→   damage to
                          behaviour   body

It follows that if at any time our feelings are negative – anxious, depressed, frustrated, hopeless – we should examine the thinking and interpretation which has led to them, to see whether that thinking was in any way faulty. If it was then we are going through negative feelings unnecessarily.

One evening, not long after I had asked for early retirement so that I could spend more time running SALT (Stress And Life Trust) and writing and running seminars, I was sitting at home reviewing my situation. Frances said to me, 'You look worried. Are you feeling anxious about anything?' 'Yes,' I said, 'I am feeling afraid in case we do not manage to make ends meet after I have given up my job.'

Frances could have said, 'I will pray for you that the Lord will give you peace.' Wisely, she did not. Instead, she asked, 'If you had a million pounds in the bank would you feel anxious?' 'Oh no', I said. Then she asked, 'Do you trust a God who owns the cattle on a thousand hills and knows whenever one sparrow falls to the ground, who says He cares for you more than the sparrows, and who has promised always to provide for you?' I paused. Frances had got me to examine my thinking and beliefs about where my security really lay – in my salary or in God Himself. Originally my thinking must have been something like: 'What if the seminars do not take off? What if I cannot get any kind of part-time work? We will have little income. How will we provide for the children? How will we survive? Our financial security totally depends upon my earning ability.' Obviously thinking of this kind had produced feelings of anxiety. Now, if I had a million pounds in the bank (thinks) then I would be secure→feelings of confidence and peace return.

Thinks – but I don't have one million in the bank, not even a thousand→more feelings of anxiety.

Do I really think that God will provide for me? – pause and think. 'He always has in the past, He has promised in His word that he will.' Decision – 'Yes I believe.' 'So why do I have to worry? – I don't!' Feelings change – the anxiety disappears – tension goes (and unknown to me – bad chemicals are replaced by good ones).

Where had my thinking been faulty? 'I will have to provide for myself and my family.' I had left God and His promises out of the reckoning. When I got my thinking right then the feelings changed – from anxiety and fear to peace and confidence, trust and excitement about the future.

Perhaps this sounds too good to be true but we promise you it works.

So the steps in any situation of anxiety or depression are:

1 To recognize and accept the feelings, not ignore or suppress or resist them. Some people, especially men and those in the caring professions and many Christians, believe that they

should never feel anxious or depressed – and so unwisely either deny it to themselves, or bottle it up, or suppress it with potentially harmful results to mind and body later. Your feelings will exist whether or not you like it, so you might as well be honest about them. It is not the feelings that are at fault, but the thinking behind them. Remember 'Unacknowledged emotions cause TROUBLE'.

2 To be clear about what the thinking has been which produced these feelings.

3 To examine the thinking as to how faulty it has been. Is it in line with biblical truth, and particularly have you left God out of the thinking?

4 To be honest with God over what you actually are thinking and believing that is a 'misbelief', and repent of it. Then to change the thinking where necessary – including putting God back into the equation. To CHOOSE to believe the truth about the situation in spite of what your feelings are. It is very difficult to take truth on board if you have not identified what the misbelief has been in the first place, and then rejected it from your thinking. The misbelief got there first, so it must be got out of the way.

There are also people who, even when things are going well, feel anxious or depressed. They are affected by thinking which is often along the lines of 'It's too good to be true', 'How long can it last?', 'What is going to spoil it?', 'I will not allow myself to enjoy this because I will only be disappointed when things change. This way I won't be surprised when they do so I will be protected against disappointment, and will have the satisfaction that I was right all along.'

Bill remembers passing the time of day with an old Scotsman in the lane near our home. He looked depressed. Trying to cheer him up I said, 'Lovely day. Isn't the weather glorious?' 'Aye,' he said, wearily, 'We shall pay for this.'

Long-standing anxiety and depression may have been associated with a lifetime of worried and depressed thinking and speaking, even during better times. These feelings can be changed too, but it will take time and effort to look consistently for the faulty thinking and keep changing it. Also, prolonged depressive thoughts and feelings will have altered the brain chemistry to such an extent that drugs may be needed to help to re-establish correct thinking patterns and kick-start the brain into producing the normal concentrations of its own chemicals after a long time of underproduction.

Prayer

Heavenly Father,

Forgive me for my faulty thinking. Forgive me especially for often leaving you out of my thinking and for worrying in some situations. Thank you for your promises and for the fact that you are always there waiting for me to include you in my thinking. I realize I need you at all times and to be in the 'thinking' about all parts of my life. Please become part of my total thinking in all situations. For Jesus's sake, Amen.

Action this day

1 Take a difficult situation that you have gone through or are going through.
2 How did you FEEL?
3 What were your thinking and beliefs about it?
4 Where was you thinking 'faulty'?
5 Did you include God in the thinking and in the equation?
6 Determine now to ask God back into the thinking.
7 Work out what your thinking is *now* – with God in the equation.

If you are often anxious and depressed, START TODAY to go through steps 1–7: about your life in general – about each situation you face.

Thoughts for today

> What a friend we have in Jesus,
> All our griefs and sins to bear.
> What a privilege to carry,
> Everything to God in prayer.
> O what peace we often forfeit!
> O what needless pain we bear!
> All because we do not carry
> *Everything* to God in prayer.

- Here I am! I stand at the door and knock. If anyone hears my voice and opens the door, I will come in and eat with him, and he with me. (Revelation 3:20)
- God is our refuge and strength, an ever-present help in trouble. Therefore we will not fear. (Psalm 46:1, 2)

Day 27

How far need we suffer negative feelings over the past, the present, the future?

Over the past three days we have been looking at the great importance of thinking and how we interpret things. The negative feelings we experience, like anxiety and depression, very often result from negative thinking which is 'faulty'. It may just be off-beam, or be very exaggerated, always pessimistic, or – and most important – leave God and His promises out of the equation.

People we see with stress problems often say to us, 'But I am a Christian. I shouldn't feel anxious or depressed. I feel guilty about this and this is making me feel even more stressed.'

But we have to acknowledge that, though born again and filled with the Spirit, we are still human. We will not be perfect until we join the Lord Jesus, and so though we need not sin because of the power of the Holy Spirit available to us, we still do. Though we need not feel anxious, we do.

Naturally and humanly speaking we will feel anxious if we are about to lose our job. We will feel sad and will want to grieve if we lose a loved one. We will feel hurt if friends let us down or reject us.

BUT WHATEVER HAPPENS, IT WILL NOT DESTROY US IF WE GET OUR THINKING RIGHT.

While is is good to get our thinking logical, rational, realistic and at least neutral if not optimistic, the way Christians think and interpret things should be fundamentally different from the way others think.

After all, we are told that we have the mind of Christ

(1 Corinthians 2:16). Non-Christians can get their thinking right, logical, rational etc., – but no more.

A number of God's basic truths should dominate and colour and be woven into our thinking about all things. If they do, then our feelings are much more likely to be those of peace rather than anxiety, joy rather than depression and patience rather than frustration. Our bodies are more likely to flourish and thrive rather than be harmed.

Let us consider some of these basic Christian truths. They concern

YOUR PAST, YOUR PRESENT AND YOUR FUTURE.

1. The past

If you have been born again (see p. 5)

YOU HAVE BEEN SAVED.

You have been given a new beginning. You have been totally forgiven. You are free of the past. It need not continue to colour your present or your future. You need not continue to feel guilty. But one word of caution here. There is a tendency around at the minute that nobody should ever feel guilty. We should not say this or that in case it makes people feel guilty. But

EVEN CHRISTIANS SHOULD FEEL GUILTY

when they have done wrong. If we do not then our consciences have been seared. Guilt should lead to a CONVICTION from the Holy Spirit that we have broken God's will and law, and spur as on to putting it right, through confessing it to God and asking for and receiving His forgiveness. Then

WE NEED NOT CONTINUE TO FEEL GUILTY.
CHRISTIANS SHOULD NOT FEEL CONDEMNED

when they have done wrong. Conviction leads us towards God and forgiveness.

Condemnation is related to us as persons. When we have done something wrong, we immediately believe that this is because we are a 'bad' person. If we believe this, there is no hope for forgiveness because we cannot change who we are. However, Christians are no longer 'bad' people, but 'saints' who have sinned, which means it is only our thoughts and actions that have to be changed, not *who* we are. It also means that God will always be willing to receive us and forgive us, no matter what it is that we have done wrong. Condemnation leads to a continuing sense of guilt and to turning away from God.

Although God forgives us, some people find it very difficult to forgive themselves. They go on fretting, blaming themselves and feeling guilty for whatever they feel they have done or not done. So although they are forgiven, the anxiety and guilt remain. If you are like this, it is essential that you

ACCEPT GOD'S FORGIVENESS BY FORGIVING YOURSELF.

If you do not, you are continuing to condemn yourself. This will work away in your mind and body, like a canker. It is also the sin of pride in that you are essentially saying 'Maybe God can forgive me, but I cannot forgive myself for falling short of MY standards and therefore I must punish myself.' What right have we to set ourselves standards that God has not, and to punish ourselves when God does not?

When you are tempted to think about those wrongdoings of the past – remember what Corrie ten Boom said:

God has put your sins at the bottom of the sea, and he has posted a sign up that says 'NO FISHING'.

2. The present

If you are born again

YOUR ARE SAFE.

Because God loves you so much, He is always on your case. He will never leave you or forsake you, never let you down. His protection surrounds you. Nothing and no one can harm you. An old chorus said

> Safe am I, safe am I,
> In the hollow of His hand.
> Sheltered o'er, sheltered o'er
> By His love for evermore.
> No foe can harm me
> No fear alarm me,
> For He keeps both day and night,
> Safe am I in the hollow of His hand.

And this is very true. So as you think about God's love and His protection, feelings of fear and anxiety will evaporate.

3. The future

Your future is assured – God has planned every moment of it. Leave it to Him. One day He will take you home to be with Him, either when He comes again or when His plans for you on earth are completed. Whatever way, that end, death or rapture will only be the beginning. The beginning of eternity with Him. No more pressures, no more stress, no more anxiety, only joy and utter fulfilment.

During their days of slavery, the negroes' lot in North America was a most unhappy one. Every day brought further trials and humiliations. They had nothing to look forward to in this life. But they had a bright clear hope for the future, and they expressed this in many of their songs. Negro spirituals are full of hope and longing and anticipation of Glory.

Nowadays, for many of us, for much of the time, life is good compared to that of the slaves. When pressures do come and we feel anxious and down, it can help to think, like the slaves, of the glorious future which awaits us. After all – our time here is very short compared to eternity with Jesus. Thoughts like those will dispel the gloom and fear, and our spirits will begin to sing.

Prayer

Lord Jesus,
Thank you for dying for me so that I can be saved, free and forgiven. Thank you for loving me and looking after me every minute of the day. This very moment, I want to place my whole life in your hands. Thank you for the plans you have for my future. I look forward to them with excitement and contentment at the same time.

Thank you for preparing a place for me with you. Because you have done this, I know that I can look forward one day to being with you. I know that I need fear nothing, not even death itself. Amen.

Action this day

1 Take time out to reflect on all that God has done for you, especially for dying for you and forgiving and saving you. Thank Him.
2 Think back to one difficult situation in your life. Can you now see God's hand in it? Thank Him.
3 Consider a present problem in your life. Remember God has it in hand. Place it firmly in His hand. Resolve to look back to this time later to see just how God led and sustained you, and then thank Him.
4 Resolve that the next time something seems overwhelming you will stop and think of God's faithfulness in the past, His present protection and love and strength. Remember that He

has plans for your future and has prepared a place for you with Him – and thank Him.

Thoughts for today

- Do not conform any longer to the pattern of this world, but be transformed by the renewing of your mind. Then you will be able to test and approve what God's perfect will is – His good, pleasing and perfect will. (Romans 12:2)
- You will keep in perfect peace him whose mind is steadfast, because he trusts in you. (Isaiah 26:3)
- Finally, brothers, whatever is true, whatever is noble, whatever is right, whatever is pure, whatever is lovely, whatever is admirable – if anything is excellent or praiseworthy – think about such things. (Philippians 4:8)
- Who shall separate us from the love of Christ? Shall trouble or hardships or persecution or famine or nakedness or danger or sword? (Romans 8:35)
- I am convinced that neither death nor life, neither angels nor demons, neither the present nor the future, nor any powers, neither height nor depth, nor anything else in all creation, will be able to separate us from the love of God that is in Christ Jesus our Lord. (Romans 8:38, 39)
- Jesus said, 'Do not let your hearts be troubled. Trust in God; trust also in me. In my Father's house are many rooms; if it were not so, I would have told you. I am going there to prepare a place for you. And if I go and prepare a place for you, I will come back and take you to be with me that you also may be where I am.' (John 14:1–3)

Ways of changing negative attitudes to positive ones

When a dog is pleased or happy it wags its tail. When we feel pleased we smile: if we are happy or amused we laugh; when down or depressed, our face becomes expressionless or sad, we speak quietly, may cry, and may sit staring into space or go off to be on our own. When we feel angry we may scowl, our chin juts out, we may speak loudly or shout. We may even lash out or at least hit one fist into the other palm or pound the desk.

When confident and courageous, we hold our head up high, brace our shoulders, take a deep breath, speak out and walk about and move purposefully. Feeling afraid or anxious, our brows furrow, our shoulders droop, we begin to scowl, we speak timidly and haltingly, may clench our teeth and fists. We may pace up and down – or slink or run away.

In other words, our feelings give rise to facial expressions, a certain way of speaking, a certain posture and ways of behaving.

We have already seen (day 24) that our feelings are a product of our thinking or interpretation or belief about events – or how we 'see' them, in our minds.

So the sequence must be something like

EVENT→THINKING→FEELINGS→EXPRESSION/SPEECH/
POSTURE/BEHAVIOUR

We have seen too that by changing our thinking, our feelings can change. However, it does appear that the sequence can also be reversed.

Experiments have been carried out in actors and actresses. If a part requires them to appear sad then they do act in this way – as far as expression, posture, speech and behaviour is concerned. There is evidence that their body chemistry and physiology begin to change, and in time they may begin to feel the part.

So it seems that by changing our expression, our posture, the way we speak and behave we can affect our feelings and body chemistry. For example, it's as if when we smile our brain is given a message that we must be pleased or happy. Norman Cousins in his book *Anatomy of an Illness*, describes how he literally laughed his way back to health from a long debilitating illness. He spent time every day with films, TV programmes and books that made him laugh. He steadily improved, felt and slept better with less pain, and eventually made a full recovery, much to the surprise of his doctors.

Laughter sessions where people are taught and encouraged to laugh together are now being incorporated into stress clinics.

So if we want to feel confident rather than afraid and anxious, an effort is required to appear, speak and act in a confident way. This in turn will affect our feelings and produce the required confidence.

Another dimension of this has to do with speech – what we say, not just the way we say it. The speech area in our brains seems to be a very powerful centre, and so what we say has a big effect on how we feel and how we behave. If we say or hear depressing, defeatist things, then we will feel and act in negative ways. On the other hand, if what we say and hear is encouraging and positive, then our expression and posture, our feelings and behaviour will follow suit.

A well-known Christian tells of a period in a community when many people were feeling down and depressed. They resolved to speak encouraging words to each other when opportunities arose. We imagine things like 'This is the day the Lord has made – I will rejoice and be glad in it', rather than 'Isn't the weather terrible?' So they began to speak out God's encouraging truths to each other, and of course to hear these truths from each other too. Within a fairly short period much of the gloom had lifted in the community, and individuals were feeling encouraged, joyful and less depressed. We cannot of course depend on everyone we meet saying positive things to us, but it is wise to seek out and try to spend some time with people who are encouragers rather than spending all our time with the negative talkers. This is particularly important if our work entails dealing with the depressed and troubled.

This is well known in marketing circles. Part of the salesman's training is teaching him all the positive things to say about his product or services, and this in turn begins to make him enthusiastic about it. But a salesman must also feel and appear confident, and part of the training in some companies is for groups of salesmen to sit and chant or shout in loud voices positive and encouraging expressions about themselves, the company and the product. I am not suggesting that we should ape this but our 'self talk' – what we say to ourselves either inwardly or out loud – can have a profound effect on how we feel and behave.

This is why constantly telling ourselves (self talk) that we are useless or worthless, that the situation is desperate and the future bleak, can have disastrous effects on our feelings, behaviour and health. But reminding ourselves – either out loud, in hymns and praise or Bible readings or prayers, or into ourselves – of God's greatness, His promises to us, His love for us, our value to Him, how we can trust Him absolutely, and how we can do all things He wants us to do through the power of His Holy Spirit, are so important in changing our feelings, behaviour and body chemistry, and making us less vulnerable to pressure.

It's as if we hear ourselves being told something or reminded of something we should have known or remembered.

The Psalms contain a lot of self talk. Psalm 103:2 has 'Praise the Lord, O my soul, and forget not all His benefits' – and all the rest of the psalm consists of the psalmist reminding himself, talking to himself about God's greatness, and justice and love.

The self talk is NOT telling ourselves we must feel better or not feel this or that – but rather is about what the facts and truth are, as in this psalm.

How we dress often affects how we feel. We dress the part –

ask any woman. But the converse also seems to apply. 'Clothes maketh the man.' It used to be, when hats were more fashionable, that a woman would cheer herself up by buying a new hat. If we are feeling down, wearing something bright can lift our feelings and spirits.

A smart and business-like suit can help us to think and feel efficient and confident. So remember to dress how you want to feel and act – not necessarily the other way round.

Prayer

Heavenly Father,
Please help me to show, through my expression, what I say and how I say it and my whole demeanour and behaviour, that I have your joy, and peace and power within me. Please help me to smile more. Please remind me to encourage myself and others by what I say, how I behave and appear. In Jesus's name, Amen.

Action this day

1 Say something positive to everyone you meet today.
2 Sing at least one song of praise.
3 Listen to one praise tape.
4 Dress how you want to feel and act.
5 Hold your head up and push your shoulders back.
6 Smile often – Jesus loves you!
7 Have a good laugh at least once a day.

Thoughts for today

- Therefore encourage one another and build each other up, just as in fact you are doing. (1 Thessalonians 5:11)
- But encourage one another daily, as long as it is called Today, so that none of you may be hardened by sin's deceitfulness. (Hebrews 3:13)
- A cheerful look brings joy to the heart, and good news gives health to the bones. (Proverbs 15:30)
- A cheerful heart is good medicine, but a crushed spirit dries up the bones. (Proverbs 17:22)
- I will be glad and rejoice in you. (Psalm 9:2)
- Do everything without complaining or arguing. (Philippians 2:14)

Day 29

An important way of protecting yourself from pressure

People who believe that whatever happens to them has a purpose are much less likely to suffer from effects of stress. They seem to take pressure in their stride.

If you think about it, this is really bound to be the case, especially if 'whatever' takes in everything, no matter how inconvenient or apparently damaging. People who think like this are likely to get less angry, or discouraged or anxious or depressed (all the kind of emotions associated with potentially 'harmful' chemicals likely to damage the body) when unexpected, annoying, downright difficult or 'bad' things happen to them. Instead, they are likely to view them as opportunities and with excitement to see what their purpose is.

It's relatively easy not to worry about some of the unpleasant things that happen to us, especially if they are not too drastic and are not likely to have a long-term effect on us.

Recently, out of the blue, one of our weekend engagements was cancelled. Even though it was for a very good reason, we were disappointed. However, very quickly we saw that suddenly and unexpectedly we were going to have the luxury of a free weekend, to rest and do whatever we pleased, as it was too late for anything else to be arranged. Since we had been extremely busy in recent weeks it was doubly welcome. It had happened, and perhaps the purpose was for us to use the time to relax and recharge our batteries. So disappointment gave place to gratitude.

It's not too difficult, too, to regain our calm and get to a position of peace when we can imagine or hope for some benefit in the future from a present difficulty.

A broken heart when we are young is not at all pleasant and is difficult to get over. But it becomes much more bearable when we get to the stage of telling ourselves, that, even if it is painful now, the purpose may be that in the future we will meet and fall in love with someone more suitable, and exciting.

But what about the really desperate things which may happen to us, the seeming catastrophes, with long-term consequences and no apparent good now or in the future? Losing our job, or health, or a loved one; failing a critical exam; the dashing of all our hopes for the future; when life seems totally unfair. Even in such circumstances, people who believe and tell themselves that there is a purpose, and that somehow it will work out well, are more likely to survive, to come through, and to succeed, despite everything.

In his book *Unlimited Powers* Anthony Robbins states that the first (of seven) beliefs of success is to do with what we have just been discovering. 'Everything happens for a reason and a purpose and it serves us.' He goes on to give examples of people who have succeeded after terrible and quite horrendous events in their lives.

How much more can and should this be true for Christians whose lives are in God's hands?

Christians are not immune from dire and tragic events in their lives. We will find times like these difficult and perplexing. We may feel down, even at the end of our tether, because this is a human reaction but

WE NEED NOT GO UNDER

if we truly believe that

GOD HAS A PURPOSE

even though WE cannot see what it can possibly be, and somehow, sometime, the good He wants and has planned will come from it.

GOD LOVES US.

Prayer

Heavenly Father,
I cannot always understand why things happen to me especially when I feel hurt badly. But I do know that you love me. You will never allow anything to happen which will be too much for me. I believe that you have a plan and purpose in everything that happens to me. One day you will let me understand. Thank you Father. Amen.

Action this day

1 Take some bad experience in your life. Can you see God's hand and plan in it? What may His purpose be for you from this event? Is there something you think you should learn from it? – if so, what?
2 If you cannot see any 'good' purpose in this or any other event in your life, remind yourself of the FACT that God has a plan which includes that event and you.

Thoughts for today

- 'For I know the plans I have for you,' declares the Lord, 'plans to prosper you and not to harm you, plans to give you hope and a future.' (Jeremiah 29:11)
- 'For my thoughts are not your thoughts, neither are your ways my ways,' declares the Lord. 'As the heavens are higher than the earth, so are my ways higher than your ways and my thoughts than your thoughts.' (Isaiah 55: 8, 9)
- Joseph said to his brothers, 'You intended to harm me, but God intended it for good to accomplish what is now being done.' (Genesis 50:20)

A difficult but highly successful way of changing pressures into opportunities

We saw yesterday that if we believe that God has a purpose in everything that happens to us and that He will use it for our good, then we will be able to face even large pressures and come through them.

Merlin Carrothers in his book *Prison to Praise* goes further than this, and although some people find it hard to accept, it is difficult to escape the biblical logic in what he writes.

As we understand it, it goes something like this.

1 IF we believe that God is sovereign, then *nothing* can happen to us, unless either God causes it to happen or allows it to happen to us. (Some people bring things on themselves, but even these are allowed by God. However, we are not talking here of self-inflicted pressures but things that happen to us, things not of our own making.)

2 If then He has caused it (however good or bad we see it) to happen or allowed it to happen, then He must have a purpose in it and it must be for our good.

3 If then He has a purpose for our good in it, should we not only be accepting it,

BUT POSITIVELY THANK AND PRAISE HIM FOR IT?

'But how on earth can I praise and thank God for . . . ? That's impossible!' I can hear you say.

Before you dismiss this concept altogether, and we know that some people have, let us try to think a little more about it.

If we ask you, 'Where do all the good things that happen to you come from?', probably you will say, 'From God' – and you have learned to thank and praise Him for them. So far so good.

If we now ask you, 'What about the hard things, the difficult, the almost impossible? Where have they come from?' You may say, 'The devil' or 'Original sin', and to some extent this is true.

However, if you believe, as we do, that God is ALL POWERFUL, and sovereign, then we can't have it both ways. If He is totally in charge, ultimately He must either have caused 'the bad' to happen to us (people sometimes forget some of the quite awful things that God actually caused to happen to people in the Bible – and not just in the Old Testament, but in the New Testament also) – or at least to have allowed it to happen. He allowed the devil to get to Job and He allowed him to 'sift' Peter.

If then, *whatever* it is God has knowingly allowed to happen to us – presumably it is for our own good because He loves us. It may be to teach us something, to reprove us, to refine us, to strengthen us – or for some reason of His own that we will never understand until we meet Him. Christ promises us that if we follow Him we will follow a path of suffering, as servants are not greater than their master, and we will have to face what He faced.

If we can acknowledge – even in theory, and even if we cannot understand it – that it must in some way be for our good, then is there not a case for not only accepting it BUT actually

PRAISING AND THANKING HIM FOR IT?

Some people find this impossible to accept and we understand this. We too found it very difficult. Some have got to the place where they feel they can thank and praise God IN the circumstances, in spite of the circumstances rather than for them. I think this is understandable.

However, we have observed that the people who say they find it most difficult to thank God FOR the circumstances are often not actually in a difficult situation at that time. What they are saying often is 'I cannot accept this teaching (in theory). I would not be able to thank God for a bad situation.' Or they are defending others: 'How could you expect someone who lost his or her job, or a loved one actually to thank and praise God for it?' Or they confuse what someone else is going through for what God is asking of them. Discussing this subject at a recent seminar, a man said, 'I have a friend who has developed dementia. Is he to thank God for that?' The question for this man, however, we think really is, 'Should I be thanking God for giving me a friend who has developed dementia?' We suspect the answer then is probably 'Yes'.

Perhaps you have not had to face any very desperate situation in your life, and you may feel that if you have to, you probably could not bring yourself to thank and praise God for it or even for allowing it. However, it may be that if that time comes, if you have to face the unthinkable, you may then be more able, and if you can it may make the difference between going through it or going under.

There are people who have had real tragedies and terrific pressures in their lives who have been able not only to accept but to begin to thank and praise God for what has happened to them.

St Paul was subjected to terrific pressure but was able to say 'in all our troubles, my joy knows no bounds' (2 Corinthians 7:4), and 'we also rejoice in our sufferings' (Romans 5:3). In the circumstances that Paul and Silas found themselves in – in prison – some of us might have been angry with God, reminding Him that we really should be out there preaching the Gospel. Others would have been believing for and claiming their deliverance. Paul and Silas were actually PRAISING GOD.

Joni Eareckson Tada writes in her book *Joni*:

I understood why Paul could 'rejoice in suffering', why James could 'welcome trials as friends', and why Peter did 'not think it strange in the testing of your faith'. All of these pressures and difficulties had ultimate positive ends and resulted in 'praise, honour and glory' to Christ . . . I can, and do, praise Him for it all – laughter and tears, fun and pain. All of it has been a part of 'Growing in grace' . . . I will speak to two thousand kids, telling them how God transformed an immature and headstrong teenager into a self-reliant young woman who is learning to rejoice in suffering.

As you know, Joni was crippled by a diving accident at seventeen, and is quadriplegic and wheelchair-bound even to this day. But how God has used her to His glory and to her blessing!

At a recent seminar we were explaining that we have been told to rejoice, praise the Lord in ALL circumstances and for all things – no matter how terrible – and that this could be of tremendous help in getting us through. At the tea interval, a man approached Bill. 'Did you know that one of the ladies sitting in the front row lost her twelve-year-old daughter a few years ago when she was murdered?' While Bill believed that what he had been saying was scriptural and true, he wondered if he had been sensitive enough in how he had put it across. He prayed that he had not hurt this dear lady. However, she too approached him later in the day. She told him that the experience of their daughter's death had been absolutely shattering. She and her husband did not know what to think or make of it. Naturally, they became depressed and confused. In time, however, they were able to bring themselves to accept that, somehow, God knew best. Their daughter was with the Lord and happy. He had a purpose even though they could not see any. He must have allowed it to happen to them. He could have protected their daughter physically. After all, we read of people in mortal danger who have prayed or have been prayed for, sometimes on the other side of the world, and God has protected them quite miraculously.

When they brought themselves to this point of acceptance they then slowly and falteringly began to thank and praise God for what He had allowed to happen to them, though they could see no purpose in it. It was then that they began to come out of the terrible depression and confusion which had surrounded them.

If you have gone through or are going through terrible events in your life, they will be painful and almost too much to bear, but they need not destroy you. If you believe that God is sovereign, that He loves you and has your good at heart, and if you can tell yourself this – then slowly you can begin to praise Him for allowing it to happen to you.

If you can get to this point, two things begin to happen. Your spirits, which have been at an all-time low, begin to rise. It also appears that sometimes it becomes easier for God to move in to change things round. This is the most powerful thing to avoid bitterness, anger and resentment towards God and circumstances. It is trust and faith in God at its most absolute level, and God works in and through our faith in Him.

You may still be sceptical. All we can say is 'Try it'. God says this is one answer, and this is how He has designed things to work. Praising and thanking God are much better for your body and mind than negative thoughts. What have you got to lose by praising God? Only your hurt, bitterness and rage. What have you got to gain? Joy, hope, confidence, patience, peace, and a crown of glory when you meet Jesus in heaven. We know which one we want to choose.

After all, what good does it do anyone or anything to stay bitter and angry and hurt? It won't change things or make them any better. It will only hurt ourselves. But praising God will make things better – even if it is only in our inner beings, but also maybe in the way God uses our faith to bring great glory and blessing to His kingdom – as with Joni. Where would she be now if she had remained bitter or simply resigned and apathetic to her injury? But look how God has used her and her injury, not just for His glory, but also for her own and millions of other people's benefit.

Prayer

Heavenly Father,

You know what I have been going through. You know how low I have felt about ....

I sometimes feel I cannot go on. It does not seem fair and I can see no reason or purpose for it. However, I believe you are sovereign and therefore must have allowed this to happen to me. I also know that you love me and that you have my highest good in mind.

And so, though it is difficult at this time, I will thank you and will go on thanking you because you know best and care so much for me. In Jesus's name, Amen.

Action this day

1 Resolve that you WILL begin to praise God for what has happened or is happening to you.
2 Resolve that in future you will praise God for ALL that happens to you. (NB. We are not suggesting that you try to ENJOY what is happening or has happened , but to thank and praise God as an act of faith in His word.)
3 Remember that one purpose we can know for sure will come out of any situation is that we are being conformed to be more like Jesus, which will last for eternity.

Thoughts for today

- And we know that in all things God works for the good of those who love Him, who have been called according to His purpose. For those God foreknew He also predestined to be conformed to the likeness of His Son, that He might be the firstborn among many brothers. (Romans 8:28, 29)
- Consider it pure joy, my brothers, whenever you face trials of many kinds, because you know that the testing of your faith develops perseverance. (James 1:2, 3)
- Do not be surprised at the painful trial you are suffering, as though something strange were happening to you. But rejoice that you participate in the sufferings of Christ. (1 Peter 4:12, 13)
- Rejoice in the Lord always. I will say it again: Rejoice! (Philippians 4:4)

PART THREE

Go on living successfully

Debriefing

Well done, you have stayed the course! We at SALT (Stress And Life Trust) would love to know how you have progressed and to encourage you.

We would value your views of this course – particularly about parts you have found most helpful, and if you feel that there are other important subjects which should have been covered.

We hope and pray that you are already beginning to enjoy living more.

To help you look forward to a whole new life which is more balanced, meaningful and satisfying, we have set out on the following pages

IMPORTANT REMINDER POINTS

for you to consider and act on.

May God continue to bless you,

Bill and Frances Munro
The Istana
Freezeland Lane
Bexhill on Sea, TN39 5JD

1 Keep up your relaxation exercises (pp. 23–25).
2 Spend some time alone with God, praising Him, thanking Him, reading His word and meditating on it (p. 8).
3 Commit the day to God. Die to self. Asked to be filled with His Holy Spirit, for His power and guidance (p. 12).
4 Take some exercise (p. 27).
5 Watch what you eat (p. 32).
6 Have a balanced day, making time for all top priorities and for relaxation and sleep (p. 56).
7 Use your time well – plan it! (p. 67).
8 Remind yourself who you are – in Christ.
   YOU BELONG, YOU ARE WORTHWHILE, YOU ARE COMPETENT (p. 77).
9 Check that your deep needs are going to be met directly from God today (p. 87).
10 Relax (p. 93).
11 Do not let the sun go down on your wrath or on unforgiveness (p. 98).
12 Resolve that your thinking will be 'good' today (p. 136).
13 Help someone in need – your good deed for the day! (p. 43).
14 If pressures come – don't panic. Go over the strategies on pp. 124–35.

Review your life regularly

1 Do you have sources of support for when you may need them? If not – start building or rebuilding (pp. 41 and 46).

2 Are your life priorities as they should be? Reorder them if necessary (p. 50).

3 Is your life 'balanced'? If necessary take steps to rebalance (pp. 56 and 62).

4 Are you using your time well? If not, replan (p. 67).

5 How is your self-image? Remember who you really are (pp. 71 and 77).

6 Where are you looking to meet your deep personal needs of security, self-worth and significance? If sources other than God have crept in – confess and rethink so that you are looking only to God for them (p. 87).

7 Is everything a rush? If you are Type 'A' – slow down, enjoy the journey, practise hints for Type 'A's (p. 93).
Regular practice of the relaxation technique is particularly important for you (pp. 23–25).

8 Is there anyone you need to forgive? Confess and forgive (p. 98).

9 Are you lonely? Get out and about if you can. Make contacts (p. 103).

10 Have you got into a rut or habit or ritual? Decide which you should break (p. 109).

11 What are your RATED goals at the minute? Are you needing to set yourself more RATED goals? (p. 114).

12 Are all your present goals under your control? If not, have you got your real overriding goals right? (p. 118).

13 Has your thinking been consistently 'good' recently? Decide to get it right, with God always included in it (p. 146).

14 Are you consistently thinking as a Christian should? Decide to get it right with regard to your past, present and future (p. 151).
15 Have your attitudes been consistently positive and encouraging? Decide to brush up on this type of behaviour (p. 157).
16 Have you been seeing 'all things' as in God's plan for you? Have you been able to praise Him for everything? (p. 162).
17 Are you doing your relaxation exercises regularly? (pp. 23–25).
    Are you keeping fit? (p. 27).

When problems and pressures come

1 Look for support (p. 46)
2 Make sure your goals are correct (p. 114).
3 Review the problem
   – How far is it self-inflicted? (p. 127).
   – Can it be solved – at least in part? (p. 128).
   – Seek advice (p. 129).
   – Act.
4 Is your thinking about the problem 'good'? (p. 136).
   Have you included God in the thinking? (p. 146).
   Change your thinking where it is faulty (p. 148).
5 Decide on a positive attitude (p. 157).
6 Is there something God wants you to learn from this problem? (p. 162).
7 Remember God's hand is in the problem. Get round to accepting it and then thanking Him for it (p. 165).

HAVE YOU GIVEN LESS THAN ALL YOUR LIFE TO GOD
OR TAKEN ANY OF IT BACK?

MAKE IT ALL OVER TO GOD – NOW – AND START
LIVING, FREE FROM THE FEAR OF STRESS.

LET GO AND LET GOD